THE $5

Chef

HOW TO
SAVE CASH
&
COOK FAST

BY MARCIE ROTHMAN

"Garlic is as good as ten mothers" from the movie by Les Blank,
Flower Films, El Cerrito, California
Eat these Words, Michael Cader, Cader Company Inc., 1991
Food for Thought: Quotations from the Kitchen, Lisa Palas,
Peter Pauper Press, 1989

ACKNOWLEDGEMENTS
My sincere and hearty thanks to everyone whose support—moral and
otherwise—helped me with the book.

Appearing in alphabetical order: Antonia Allegra, Harrah Argentine, Terry
and Wendy Bachman, Elizabeth Bertani, Fred Brack, Judith Bronowski, Mark
Charnas, Elaine Corn, Larry Dietz, Mark and Soleil Donahue, Susan Hoyer,
Mark Loffler, Grant Loucks, Kate Newkirk, Tara O'Leary, Alison Pollock,
Paula Romich, Dell Schilleci, Sahedran Shelborne, Dawn Simms, Jason Squire,
Karen Stabiner, Marilou Vaughan, Dennis Yeast, Beryl Zimberoff, and anyone
I inadvertently missed, thank you.

With extra special thanks to:
Karl Fleming (who named me "The $5 Chef")
Buttitta Design (logo and cover)
Dena Kaye (my dearest and best friend)
KOVR-TV (everyone...including Dewey Hopper and my terrific production crew)
Lucy Nielsen (book design, production...and patience)
Leo Pearlstein (who started me on TV, years ago)
Ray and Shirley Rothman (my parents, who began the whole thing)
Rita Rothman (my sister with an amazing eye for clarity)
Kit Snedaker (editing and encouragement)
Francine Thistle (proofreading)
Baron Wolman (my everpresent muse)

to grandma julia, who filled my life with sage advice and my tummy with good food.

table of contents

preface

I've always loved to eat good food. Early on I learned from my mother and her mother that good food is neither expensive nor difficult to make.

Growing up in Southern California I ate lots of corn, tomatoes and strawberries picked from the fields near our house and sold from roadside stands and supermarkets. We always ate simple meals—except when my mother enthusiastically embraced a new cuisine. When she learned to cook French, we went through a period of hollandaise, bearnaise, and bordelaise until we hit sauce malaise. The Cuisinart phase followed the French, and foods were either shredded or pureed while mom learned to use the machine.

My grandmother taught me to cook without a formal recipe. I learned to touch the dough to feel if there was enough flour and to taste the tomato sauce to see if it needed just a pinch more sugar to counterbalance the tomatoes' acid. It seemed that every time we made coffee cake the number of eggs changed, but I got to know the proper consistency of dough for the most ethereal of cakes.

I've always had unconventional eating styles. As a kid my idea of breakfast heaven was leftovers ...hamburger, chicken, vegetables, even cold mashed potatoes. I'd sit at the table gnawing on a chicken bone while my family chuckled as they ate Rice Krispies and oatmeal.

I carried this leftover habit to my best friend Dena's house, where her father used to prepare some of the best Chinese food this side of Hong Kong. I lived for the leftovers in their refrigerator.

I used to count calories in my sleep, a result of my passion for food. Then, more than ten years ago, I decided to make weight watching easier and began cooking low-salt, lowfat meals with robust overtones of all ethnic cuisines I knew, including Chinese, Indian, and French. In order to see my friends—most of whom were on some sort of health kick or fad diet—I gave dinner parties. The challenge was to make a fabulous meal that suited everyone's diet of the moment including, but not limited to, no salt, no meat, only meat, only fruit, no carbohydrates. There were a few skeptics the first time I served soy sauce on the side (to be added according to individual preference) instead of adding it to the recipe. Friends later confessed the food tasted wonderful. No one ever turned down an invitation to eat low-sodium, lowfat Chinese or Indian food at my house.

It was a childhood friend, Kate, who taught me that not everyone learns to cook while growing up. Kate's mom was the quintessential "I Hate to Cook" cook. She made fabulous tacos and that was it. Years later, Kate told me she wanted to learn to cook in my style: open the refrigerator and use what was there to create a dish, with or without a written recipe. We talked about how she could learn to cook. She confessed to something I call kitchen anxiety: fear of cooking, of making a mistake on a dish or worse yet, not understanding a recipe. Kate's anxiety was fueled by the common notion that every recipe is set in concrete, never to have one ingredient change by so much as a pinch. Her inability to trust her own taste kept Kate from cooking much of anything beyond those wonderful tacos she learned from her mom.

That lunch with Kate was pivotal for me—it launched the first phase of my professional cooking career. I worked with kitchen-anxious cooks to make them more comfortable in their kitchens and taught them—long before it was fashionable—to cook with no salt and less fat.

Then came my television segments. For the past eight years, I've appeared on KOVR-TV (ABC) in Sacramento, California. These weekly, live, three-minute shows carry my message: Preparing delicious, fresh food is easy and saves money.

Realizing that most of us are on a tight food budget, I began the second phase of my creative cooking career, and three years ago became **THE $5 CHEF**. Now I look for ways to shop wisely and cook innovatively on a weekly food budget of about $120 for a family of four. That's roughly $5 a meal.

The essence of my book is this: You can make great food without going broke—and you can have a good time doing it.

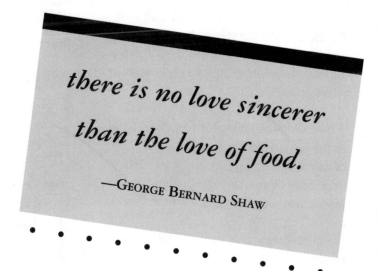

there is no love sincerer than the love of food.

—GEORGE BERNARD SHAW

introduction

QUESTION: Can $5 buy a meal for four people? Answer: Yes, and not just spaghetti. For many, grocery shopping means balancing on a budgetary tightrope. Once home, cooking can be equally challenging. Just look at Cathy as portrayed by cartoonist Cathy Guisewite.

Many of us have questions about recipe terms and techniques. In this book the recipes have simple explanations so they're easy to follow, and there's room for substitutions and improvisations according to individual tastes. Recipes are organized alphabetically by major ingredient from apples to zucchini and are cross-referenced for minimum page-flipping. For example, all chicken recipes are found under "Chicken" rather than under the usual entree or appetizer listing. They are also indexed according to type of dish. There's a section on how to add dash to a dish with the use of cupboard staples, herbs, and spices. Short appendices give down-to-earth explanations of cooking terms and other basic information.

CATHY by Cathy Guisewite

A dwindling food budget coupled with a trip to the grocery store is enough to give most of us the how-to-save-money jitters. This book gives money-saving shopping tips, menus, and shows what labels mean. A supermarket map helps steer you away from budget-busting foods. By shopping wisely, you'll be able to splurge occasionally on expensive ingredients.

If creating great meals on a budget seems an impossible task, just look at my friend Dell who feeds four kids and two adults on $120 a week. Though she's short on time, she doesn't serve fast foods or sweet snacks. In fact, she spends 45 minutes max in the kitchen making dinner using mostly fresh ingredients. And yes, a microwave helps cut cooking time, but it isn't a must.

THE $5 CHEF: HOW TO SAVE CASH & COOK FAST explains how to shop strategically for one or a crowd, cook quickly and imaginatively, and save time, money and health.

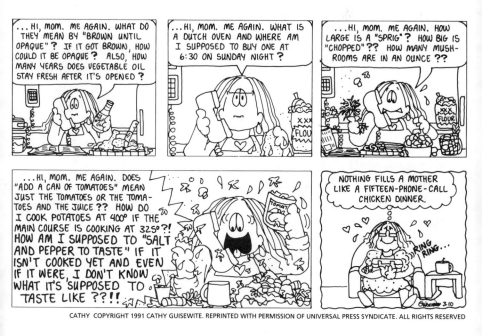

CATHY COPYRIGHT 1991 CATHY GUISEWITE. REPRINTED WITH PERMISSION OF UNIVERSAL PRESS SYNDICATE. ALL RIGHTS RESERVED

BEFORE MARKETING

Money-Saving Tips for Menu Planning

◆ Is a meal a bite grabbed at the kitchen sink or in the car? Is the kitchen a restaurant in disguise, where everyone cooks and eats something different at the same meal? Are there special dietary needs such as lowfat, choles-terol, sodium and sugar? Consider your **EATING LIFESTYLE** which means time available to cook, food likes and dislikes and dietary needs.

◆ Plan **MENUS** with as much fresh produce, meat and dairy as possible. Fresh foods usually cost less than "budget busters"—those prepackaged, boxed and prepared frozen foods that may not even be as quick to make as their fresh counterpart.

◆ Different **DISHES** work for different lifestyles: Quick raw salads, fruits and vegetables work for a busy cook. Make-ahead casseroles, stews, and freezer dishes or quick meals of fresh foods work well for week-end cooks.

◆ Plan **A WEEK'S WORTH OF MEALS** for greater confidence and speed in the market. Shop once or twice a week.

◆ Consider **PLANNED-OVERS** (foods used for more than one meal, fresh or frozen) that take advantage of larger cuts of meat and store specials.

◆ Always use a **SHOPPING LIST** even if you've never done it before. The list is a guide for menu planning and organizing: shopping is faster and more efficient. A list eliminates the temptation to "cruise" the aisles picking up costly impulse items. It avoids duplication of items already on hand. Overbuying (parti-cularly of fresh fruits and vegeta-bles), plays havoc with a budget when excess fresh food spoils and goes to waste.

Quick Tips Before Shopping

◆ Read newspaper **FOOD ADS** for specials on meats, produce and basic packaged goods (peanut butter, tomato sauce, ketchup, etc.), so menus reflect good buys.

◆ Shop in one place and avoid the **"SUPERMARKET HOP"** (going from market to market for a bargain here—a bargain there). Supermarket hopping not only wastes time and money in the market, but increases transportation costs as well.

◆ Avoid **CONVENIENCE STORES** for shopping. They are good in a pinch but expensive. Use **WAREHOUSE STORES** for bulk food bargains.

◆ Check **CUPBOARD** to replenish such staples as pasta, rice, tomato sauce, spices.

◆ Recycle **LEFTOVERS** for use in the next few meals.

◆ Check product **COUPONS**. They may save money on favorite brands, though many times a market special on a less expensive, higher quality product is a better buy. Consider **GENERIC** brands for price and quality. Coupons are rarely offered for fresh produce or meats.

to chew on

Not long ago a mother and her young son were shopping in a supermarket. The child, trying to be helpful, picked up a package and brought it to her. "Oh no, honey," protested the mother. "Go put it back. You have to cook that." —INDIANAPOLIS NEWS

• • • • • • •

SAMPLE MENUS FOR FOUR

These menus shows how to use most of the food on the Sample Shopping List in the Appendix. Use them as a guide and adapt to dietary needs and lifestyle. An asterisk (*) means recipe is included in the book.

Breakfast   All breakfasts include fresh fruit or juice, toast or cereal; with eggs or an omelette, bacon or pancakes as a once-a-week meal.

◆ **DAY ONE**

Lunch   Bacon, Lettuce and Tomato Sandwiches; Carrot Soup*; Graham Crackers.

Dinner   Fish with Vegetables and Rice*; Green Salad; Sauteed Bananas*.

◆ **DAY TWO**

Lunch   Peanut Butter and Jelly Sandwiches; Fruit.

Dinner   Roast Chicken*; Spinach Salad; Banana Squash; Potatoes; Baked Apples*.

◆ **DAY THREE**

Lunch   Tortillas with Melted Cheese; Fruit.

Dinner   Vegetable Stir-Fry with Rice; Applesauce.

◆ **DAY FOUR**

Lunch   Asian Flavored Pasta Salad*; Oatmeal cookies.

Dinner   Grilled or Roasted Lamb*; Vegetable; Mashed Potatoes*; Green salad; Spiced Apple Cake*.

to chew on

Many of these dishes travel well and convert easily into bagged lunches. Bringing lunch from home ensures you'll eat well while saving money.

• • • • • • •

DAY FIVE

Lunch   Caesar Potato Salad*;
Fresh Fruit.

Dinner   Lamb Fajitas*; Tortillas;
Green Salad; Fresh Fruit.

◆ DAY SIX

Lunch   Confetti Rice Salad*;
Fresh Fruit.

Dinner   Roast Turkey; Potatoes;
Salad; Chocolate Angel Food
Cake*.

◆ DAY SEVEN

Lunch   Turkey Sandwiches;
Orange Oatmeal Chews*.

Dinner   Pasta Casserole*; Salad;
No-Bake Peach Pie*.

Party Menus

THANKSGIVING FOR EIGHT
Carrot Soup*; Roasted or Barbecued
Turkey or Chicken with Mushroom
Gravy*; Stuffing; Restuffed Baked
Potatoes with Artichoke Hearts*;
Vegetable; Cranberry Salad*;
Pumpkin Custard*.

NEW YEAR'S FOR EIGHT
Chicken with Red Wine*; Salad or
Vegetable; Potatoes, Rice, Pasta or
Bread; Almond Meringue Pie*.

ANY OCCASION BUFFET FOR TWELVE
Filo Kisses*; Spicy Chicken*;
Polenta*; Salad or Vegetable;
Bread; Fruit; Chocolate Truffles*.

to chew on

Easy, healthful snacks include
such foods as popcorn (not the
pre-flavored convenience variety), carrots, celery sticks, and
fruit.

AT THE MARKET

Money-Saving Shopping Tips

◆ **BE FLEXIBLE** in meal planning—it's no bargain to buy produce, meat or dairy that isn't fresh. At the market, be prepared to make ingredient substitutions to avoid higher prices or anything past its prime.

◆ At the supermarket, notice where the **FRESH DAIRY, MEAT, BREADS AND PRODUCE SECTIONS** are—usually the sides of the market. Begin shopping in these areas rather than the inner aisles where many "budget-busters" (high-priced convenience foods) are found.

◆ **IMPULSE BUYING** from hunger pangs or a screaming child can fill a cart with such expensive pre-packaged "instant" convenience, snack and processed foods as chips, cookies, microwave popcorn, rice mixes and frozen entrees. These foods dent a budget in less time than it takes to open the package.

◆ Look for nuts, pastas, grains, candies, and cookies sold loose in **BULK**. It's easier to buy smaller quantities and prices are lower than similar prepackaged foods.

◆ End-of-the-aisle food displays may not always be cheaper. Compare prices with different sizes or other brands of the same item.

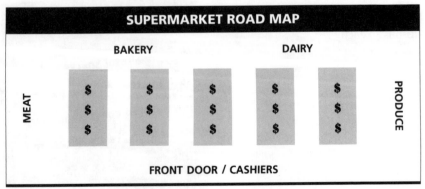

SUPERMARKET ROAD MAP

BAKERY   DAIRY

MEAT   PRODUCE

$ $ $ $ $ $ $ $ $ $ $ $ $ $ $

FRONT DOOR / CASHIERS

$$$ show where budgets are busted on canned, boxed and frozen foods. Shop inner aisles for cupboard staples such as tomato sauce, tuna, juices, grains, herbs, spices, and peanut butter.

AVOID THESE FOODS WHENEVER POSSIBLE.

NOT ONLY ARE THEY BUDGET-BUSTERS, THEY MAY INCREASE SUGAR, SALT AND FAT IN A MEAL:

✔ OUT OF SEASON FRESH FRUITS AND VEGETABLES

✔ SAUCED AND SEASONED FROZEN VEGETABLES

✔ SUGAR-COATED CEREALS

✔ READY-MADE OR READY-TO-BAKE COOKIES, CAKES, PIES AND BUNS

✔ FROZEN PREPARED FOODS

✔ POTATO, CORN OR CHEESE CHIPS AND PUFFS, READY-MADE DIPS

✔ SOFT DRINKS

✔ CANDY

✔ HIGH FAT DAIRY PRODUCTS SUCH AS CHEESE AND ICE CREAM

VEGETABLES

◆ **RULE OF THUMB:** A pound serves 3 to 4.

◆ Buy produce in season. For example, in winter buy spaghetti squash (a winter variety) that has better flavor and costs less than zucchini (a summer squash).

◆ Spend about 69 cents a pound for produce in season. (Some average nationwide prices in January, 1991, were white potatoes at 33 cents a pound and bananas at 44 cents a pound.)

◆ Look for fresh produce on special (the weekly food ads are important here).

◆ Look for day-old produce packaged separately. Depending on quality, it's a good buy for higher-priced produce.

◆ Year-round, high-priced vegetables such as fresh mushrooms can be included in menus because a few of them sliced go a long way.

AT THE MARKET

POULTRY

◆ **RULE OF THUMB:** A whole fryer feeds 4. Cooked and shredded, chicken can be stretched when added to other such ingredients as lettuce, vegetables, beans or rice.

◆ Poultry specials: Buy whole chickens or parts—legs or breasts—in bulk. Use backs and necks for chicken stock, breasts for stir-fry and legs and thighs for another meal. Cut the poultry at home with a good knife or poultry shears—it's easy and a money-saver.

Hints for cutting up a whole bird

With bird on its back, gently pull wings and thighs/legs away from body and cut skin to expose joints. Cut wings first, at joint attached to body. Then cut thighs/legs. Cut between rib joints to separate back from breast. To split breast, lay skin-side down and make a small cut at top of breast in white cartilage near wish bone. Remove brown bone (keel) from the meat.

◆ Compare the cost of a whole 3-pound chicken at $.79 a pound with a pound of boned, skinned breasts at $3.75 a pound. The difference is considerable.

◆ Use whole turkeys or parts. Turkey is available year-round.

◆ Ground turkey is low in fat and substitutes easily for other ground meats.

MEAT

◆ **RULE OF THUMB:** A pound of meat serves 3 to 4 people, 3 to 4 ounces each, depending on fat and water content. Look for percentage of fat per pound in ground meat. Low-priced ground beef may have high fat, so it's not always a wise buy.

◆ Use meat as a side dish, rather than a main course. It saves money. Vegetables, pastas and rice are healthier main attractions.

◆ Watch for specials on meats. If it's convenient and a good deal, buy larger cuts of beef, lamb or pork and freeze for later meals. Generally, weekly store specials allow for one or two meat meals a week without going over budget. Good steaks or roasts can be included with a watchful eye on prices.

◆ Stretch expensive cuts of meat. For example, only a little pork or beef is needed for a stir-fry if mixed with vegetables.

◆ Consider buying a bigger cut of meat such as a chuck roast, to process at home into hamburger and other dishes.

SEAFOOD

◆ **RULE OF THUMB:** A pound serves 4, approximately 4 ounces each.

◆ It's a good low-calorie protein source, cooks quickly with little waste.

◆ Look for seafood specials on high ticket items such as shrimp. Buy a few and stretch by cutting in pieces.

◆ If fish smells at all fishy or like ammonia, then it's over the hill.

◆ Fresh frozen fish means it has been previously frozen just hours after it's caught, then sold thawed. It should be labeled previously frozen. Fresh frozen is readily available to buy and may cost less than fresh.

◆ Fresh whole fish have clear, full eyes, bright red or pink gills, moist shiny skin and firm, elastic flesh that bounces back to the touch.

◆ Soft, mushy flesh is a sign of age and refrozen thawed fish.

BAKERY

◆ Look for day-old breads and bakery products at the supermarket or at bakery outlet stores. Day-old bread is good for homemade croutons.

$ AT THE MARKET

Raw Rice
Ingredients: Rice

Convenience Rice
Ingredients: Enriched rice, salt, food starch, modified natural flavors, sugar, chicken fat, onions, monosodium glutamate, chicken broth, dried chicken, dried parsley, dried yeast, soy flour, dried garlic, spices, partially hydrogenated vegetable oil (soy or cotton seed, etc.)

Ingredients

Read the labels—ingredients are listed according to amount, with the most first and the least last. Notice cooking time of processed food. It may be as long or longer than for fresh food. Compare, for example, a bag of raw rice and the boxed, seasoned, convenience variety. Raw is just rice. It's cheaper, takes the same 20 minutes to cook and can be seasoned to taste.

Unit Pricing

Take advantage of unit pricing labels on the shelves of most supermarkets. Unit pricing is the cost per ounce, pound, pint, or other measure, for a specific food product. Read the label, compare prices of generic brands as well as package sizes, and the cost of prepackaged and convenience foods versus the fresh food equivalent.

Open Dating

Open dating is the date the store must remove or sell the item. Look for manager's specials on meat and dairy products past their "Pull-by" or "Sell-by" date (the date the store must remove or sell the item). Similarly, look for blemished or day-old fruits and vegetables at reduced prices. Buy these items only if they will be used. They won't keep and it could mean thowing food and money down the drain.

PRE-PACKAGED HERBED RICE

APPROXIMATE COST:

1 7.2-ounce package $1.25

= 17.2¢ per ounce

YIELD: 7 1/2-cup servings
TOTAL COST: $1.25 to serve 7

THE ALTERNATIVE TO PRE-PACKAGED HERBED RICE

APPROXIMATE COST:

2 pounds raw rice $1.35

= 4.2¢ per ounce

Additional flavorings (i.e., onion, herbs, olive oil) 80¢

YIELD: 32 1/2-cup servings
TOTAL COST: $2.15 to serve 32

TRICKS FROM THE CUPBOARD

Add Dash to a Dish with Herbs and Spices

How many times has the sight of yet another tuna casserole or chicken à la anything created mutiny at the dinner table? The dreary monotony of the same foods over and over again is enough to send the hungriest diners to the nearest hamburger joint.

Break the pattern with different herbs, spices and other flavors such as vinegars and mustards. An easy way to use flavors is to ask the same question many of us do when choosing a restaurant, "What am I in the mood for—Italian, Chinese, American, or Mexican?" Once that's determined, it's easier to know what herbs and spices to use. Refer to the following list of spices in ethnic categories. Many overlap. Jazzing up a chicken, Chinese-style, for instance, is easy. Use sesame oil, ginger and garlic and then roast or barbecue.

Garlic is as good as ten mothers.

—LES BLANK

Spicing Hints

◆ Pick one or two flavors, use a pinch in the recipe and then taste.

◆ Add more spice or another flavor if the food seems too bland.

◆ Garlic is universal in every cuisine and it works well with other herbs, spices and flavors.

◆ Fresh garlic, onion, ginger, parsley and cilantro give more punch to food than their dried equivalent.

◆ Look for fresh herbs in the produce section.

◆ Rinse and dry fresh herbs. Refrigerate in plastic, or with stems in water, covered with a plastic bag.

◆ Instead of one flavor, try dried herb seasonings such as Italian, Mexican, Chinese, Indian or French.

◆ To increase the flavor of dried herbs, crush them in your hand, then add to food.

◆ Check the spice chart. Too many flavors overpower the subtle taste of fresh ingredients.

◆ Spices are good salt substitutes.

◆ Foods may taste bland, particularly if salt is limited. Check the spice chart to jazz up flavors.

◆ When cooking, taste the food to adjust the seasoning.

◆ No dash to a dish? Try a squeeze of lemon juice, zest of orange or lemon, a drop or two of vinegar, Tabasco or Worcestershire, a pinch of cayenne, or freshly ground pepper or salt.

◆ Too much salt in a finished dish? Try a pinch of sugar or a dash of lemon juice or vinegar.

Herb Mixtures

FINE HERBS: A mixture of tarragon, parsley, chives, and other specified fresh or dried herbs.

BOUQUET GARNI: Bay leaf, thyme, parsley and an onion with one or two whole cloves stuck in it. The herbs can be fresh or dried and tied in a cheesecloth for easy removal (and disposal) after cooking.

FIVE-SPICE POWDER: Typically star anise, fennel, Szechwan peppercorns, cloves and cinnamon.

GARAM MARSALA: Usually cardamom, black pepper, cumin, coriander, cinnamon, and cloves.

	Allspice	Basil	* Bay leaf	Black bean sauce	Black beans, salted	Capers	Celery seed	* Cayenne	Chives	Cilantro/coriander	Chiles	* Cinnamon	Cloves	Coconut	* Cumin	* Curry powder	* Dill	Fennel seed	Fish sauce (nam pla)	Five spice powder
AMERICAN	•	•	•			•	•	•			•	•	•				•	•		
CHINESE				•	•					•	•	•						•		•
FRENCH	•		•			•			•								•	•		
INDIAN			•							•	•	•	•		•	•		•		
ITALIAN		•	•			•												•		
MEXICAN	•		•						•		•	•	•	•		•				
SOUTH-EAST ASIAN		•								•	•	•			•	•	•		•	

* Herbs and spices to always have on hand. This chart is a general guide. Feel free to create your own combinations.

Garam masala	* Garlic	* Ginger	Hoisin sauce	Lemon	Lemon grass	Lime	Mint	Mustard or seed	Nutmeg	Orange zest	* Oregano	Paprika	Parsley	* Rosemary	Sage	Sesame seeds	Sesame oil	Star anise	Soy	Tamarind	Tarragon	* Thyme	Turmeric
	•			•		•	•	•	•	•	•	•	•	•	•						•	•	•
	•	•	•					•		•						•	•	•	•				
	•							•	•	•	•		•	•							•	•	
•	•	•				•	•	•	•			•								•			•
	•						•		•	•	•	•	•	•	•						•	•	
	•					•				•							•			•			
	•	•		•	•	•	•													•			•

TRICKS FROM THE CUPBOARD

Footnotes for Select Herbs and Spices

◆ ALLSPICE: Dried small berries that taste and smell like cinnamon, nutmeg and cloves. Toss a few whole in pot roast for a subtle flavor or put a ground pinch in spice cake or on banana squash.

◆ ANISE SEED: Tiny licorice-flavored seeds much like fennel. Use in cookies, sauces, stews, fish and shellfish.

◆ BASIL: Fresh or dried, its flavor is minty and slightly peppery. Add to meats, poultry, vegetables, pasta, salads or rice.

◆ BAY LEAF: A pungent, aromatic leaf that adds subtle taste and fragrance to stews, sauces and soups.

◆ FENNEL SEED: Lovers of licorice adore fennel. Fresh (a green bulb), it's eaten raw in salads or cooked as a side dish. As a seed, it flavors Italian sausage, Chinese five-spice and Indian curry powders.

◆ GARLIC: A head of fresh garlic consists of many cloves (not the tiny black pungent spice used on ham). Buy uniformly white or light purple and white bulbs (color denotes variety, not flavor) with no soft or black spots. Always buy loose heads; it's bad manners to take a few cloves. Store in a cool dry place with good ventilation. Plastic bags create moisture that rots the garlic. To peel a clove, loosen skin by smashing garlic with the flat side of a knife.

◆ GINGER: Pungent, hot and distinctive, use it in baking, curries and stir-frys. Chopped, grated or sliced, a little goes a long way. Store refrigerated in a covered jar filled with white wine or sherry. Or freeze for about a month, wrapped in plastic. To use frozen, cut undefrosted pieces as needed. Store and use with or without its skin—I prefer unpeeled because its essence is just below the skin. For desserts and some Oriental foods, use crystallized, preserved or pickled ginger.

The Staples

Imaginative twists on routine dishes, as well as ingredients for last-minute meals, depend on staples in the cupboard. These pantry items include common staples and exotic ones easily found in ethnic sections of supermarkets. Watch for specials on favorite brands. The recipes show new ways to use these ingredients.

FRESH

◆ Onions, garlic, ginger, parsley.

◆ Lemons, oranges, limes: juice or zest (the finely grated peel) gives a gentle flavor nudge to just about any dish.

◆ Eggs: Whites are protein and great for angel food cake; yolks are fat and cholesterol—use sparingly.

DAIRY

◆ Milk, cheese, yogurt, butter or margarine: Mix lowfat plain yogurt with mayonnaise to substitute for higher fat and calorie regular mayonnaise.

DRY

◆ Pasta, noodles, rice: Buy unseasoned; keeps almost indefinitely. Chinese cellophane (bean thread) noodles: For soup, salad or stir-fry.

◆ Beans and legumes: Pinto, black, great northern, lima, garbanzo, lentils, split peas.

◆ Flour: All-purpose unbleached white. Sugar: white, brown, powdered. Salt, chocolate chips, unsweetened cocoa.

◆ Flavored extracts such as vanilla, almond and lemon.

TRICKS FROM THE CUPBOARD

CANNED/BOTTLED

◆ Tomato sauce, tomato paste and ketchup.

◆ Garbanzos, kidney beans.

◆ Tuna and anchovies.

◆ Sauces: Barbecue, hoisin (Chinese sweet and salty for poultry or vegetables).

◆ Chicken and beef broth: Look for low-sodium variety.

◆ Olives.

◆ Salsas or chile sauces.

◆ Jellies and jams, jalapeño or fruit.

◆ Mustards: In addition to the usual ballpark variety, try mustard flavored with shallots, honey or whole mustard seeds. Dried mustard powder adds heat to a dish without the vinegar pungency of the bottled mustards.

◆ Olive and vegetable oil.

◆ Non-stick spray: Use instead of butter or oil to prevent sticking. Comes plain or olive oil flavored.

◆ Vinegars: Varieties include rice, wine, sherry, raspberry, balsamic, white and cider. If a dish tastes bland, try a dash of vinegar.

◆ Wine: Look for specials on such varietals as Cabernet Sauvignon, Zinfandel, Sauvignon Blanc, Chenin Blanc, Chardonnay.

◆ Juices: Tomato, V-8 (for entrees and sauces), apple and pineapple (for baking, poaching or sauces). Clam juice: For seafood sauces and dishes.

◆ Raisins: A natural sweetener in fruit chutneys, and in sauces with such spices as cumin, ginger, garlic and cinnamon. Good for texture and color.

◆ Marinated artichoke hearts: Great for frittatas (egg pancakes), salads, or with meats and poultry.

NUTS

◆ Unsalted peanuts, walnuts and almonds. Peanut butter.

◆ Water chestnuts: Add crunch to a vegetable, salad, or egg dish.

FROZEN

◆ Juice concentrates like apple and orange.

◆ Bulk frozen vegetables: Peas, green beans and corn make colorful additions to rice or pasta salad, a side dish or a casserole.

to chew on

REMEMBER

For quick cooking instructions, use recipes on backs of packages.

RECIPES

How To Personalize Your Cooking

◆ Ever make a sandwich with mustard but no mayonnaise? Or create a salad from leftovers? Or heat up a bottled spaghetti sauce and add an extra dash of oregano?

If so, you have learned how to PER-SONALIZE A RECIPE. Quality of ingredients, differences in measuring, and individual cooking style alter every recipe. Use more (or less) of an ingredient, add (or delete) an ingredient, or even present the dish differently to change the recipe. Trust your personal food preferences, and your senses—taste, smell, sight and touch. The only way you can truly ruin food is to burn or oversalt it. The recipes in this book are flexible; use them as guides.

Good food relies on good ingredients rather than expensive cookware and gadgets. A quick word about COOKING UTENSILS: I still use the same pots and pans I've had for years. In fact, many belonged to my grandmother, and they still work just fine. The most important utensils in my kitchen are a few sharp knives (a large chef's size and a small, thin, serrated vegetable knife), my garlic press, a stainless steel grater, a saucepan, and a cast iron or non-stick skillet. Cooking in a MICROWAVE OVEN with ceramic or glass dishes eliminates the need for an arsenal of traditional metal pots and pans. Many of these recipes are easily adaptable to microwave cooking.

Sometimes I measure ingredients with my eye and hand or a convenient soup spoon or coffee cup.

ROUGH MEASURING EQUIVALENTS

HANDFUL = 3/4 to 1 cup

SPLASH = 1 to 2 tablespoons

PINCH = 1/8 to 1/4 teaspoon

GENEROUS PINCH = 1 teaspoon

DASH = A pinch

SOUP SPOON = 1 tablespoon

MUG OR COFFEE CUP = 3/4 to 1 cup

WINE GLASS = 3/4 to 1 cup

tips for healthful cooking

♦ **To lower cholesterol:** Omit or cut down EGG YOLKS (cholesterol). Use egg whites (protein) or egg substitutes.

♦ **To lower fat:** Cut down on SATURATED FATS (mayonnaise, coconut and palm oils, butter, sour cream, cheese, and meat) and use lowfat or nonfat yogurt, light sour cream, mayonnaise and buttermilk. Reduce the higher fat ingredients by stretching them with the lower and nonfat varieties.

Use cheese as a condiment, rather than a main ingredient.

When the recipe says cook in oil or butter, use a well-seasoned pan and less fat than indicated. Or use a non-stick pan with a non-stick spray; poach in a little liquid such as broth, water, wine or a combination (perfect for fish and chicken); flavor the poaching liquid with a small amount of oil or butter; broil meat so the fat drips off; steam meats, fish, and poultry on a bed of vegetables with liquid; use the microwave oven.

If a recipe says add cream or butter to the sauce and EVERY CALORIE COUNTS, try a dash of wine, a splash of wine vinegar, a squeeze of lemon, or if there are vegetables in the sauce, puree them to flavor and thicken the sauce.

♦ **To lower sodium:** If salt is a problem and the recipe calls for more than a pinch, SKIP THE SALT. Try variations of herbs and spices or salt-free seasonings that add great zing to food. Don't forget Worcestershire and Tabasco sauce, Angostura bitters, low- or no-salt mustard, even light soy (which can be diluted with water), and zest of lemon, lime or orange.

For medical questions, see a doctor and check with the American Heart Association HEART HEALTHY GUIDELINES.

Most of these recipes are low in fat, cholesterol and sodium.

SAVORY BAKED APPLES

Serves 4

◆ Baked apples are versatile—use them sweet for dessert or savory with meat and poultry. Try this easy side dish with roast pork or turkey. It can cook in the oven with the meat.

4 large tart baking apples, cored and trimmed to stand upright

1 cup prepared stuffing mix or bread crumbs

1/4 onion, finely chopped

4 tablespoons carrot, finely shredded

4 medium mushrooms, finely diced

2 tablespoons raisins, optional

2 tablespoons walnuts, finely chopped, optional

1 teaspoon dried Italian herbs, or a mixture of basil, thyme, oregano

1 tablespoon fresh parsley, finely chopped

Black pepper, to taste

1 tablespoon butter, optional

1/2 cup water, apple juice, or white wine

1. Carefully hollow out the apples to enlarge the stuffing cavity. Mix together the remaining ingredients, except butter and liquid, and stuff apples. Top each apple with a dot of butter.

2. Place in baking dish with water, apple juice or wine. Cover and bake in preheated 350 degree oven for 30 to 40 minutes or until apples are soft. Or cook in the microwave oven according to manufacturer's instructions.

VARIATIONS: For dessert, instead of savory stuffing, use a mixture of 1 teaspoon ground allspice or cinnamon, 2 tablespoons sugar, and 1/4 cup each raisins and walnuts, chopped together.

Make applesauce by cooking cut apples in a saucepan or microwave with a little sugar, cinnamon and half an orange.

SEE ALSO Bananas Sauteed and Chicken Livers with Apple and Onion.

APPLE-CELERY CHUTNEY

Serves 6 to 8

◆ Chutneys, like salsas, complement grilled and roasted poultry and meats. They are a colorful interplay of flavor and texture. Other fruits such as bananas, peaches or pears can be substituted. Unlike many chutneys, this one is not cooked so it can be made in minutes.

3 tart apples, cored and diced

3 stalks celery, diced

1/2 cup raisins

1 heaping teaspoon fresh ginger, finely grated

Juice of 1 large lemon or lime

1 tablespoon onion, finely grated, or to taste

1 tablespoon sugar, or to taste

1. Mix all ingredients in a bowl adding lemon juice, onion and sugar to taste.

2. Refrigerate. Will keep refrigerated for about 1 week if tightly covered.

SEE ALSO Corn-Raisin Chutney.

SPICED APPLE CAKE

Serves 6

◆ An easy-to-make spiced fruit cake that works as well for the budget as it does for the waistline: it's low in cost and fat. Serve luke-warm or at room temperature.

1 egg plus 1 egg white

1/4 cup lowfat milk

2/3 cup sugar

1-1/2 cups flour

Pinch salt

1/4 teaspoon each ground cinnamon
   and cloves, to taste, optional

2 pounds apples, pears or a mixture
   of both, peeled, cored and sliced

Zest of 1 lemon

9-inch pie or cake pan, greased
   and floured

1 tablespoon butter, optional

1. In a large bowl beat eggs with milk. Add sugar and continue to beat.

2. Add flour, salt and spices and mix well. Dough will be thick. Add fruit and zest. Mix so fruit is well coated.

3. Pour into prepared cake pan and dot with butter if desired. Bake in preheated 350 degree oven until top is lightly browned, approxi-mately 35 to 40 minutes.

4. Serve at room temperature or lukewarm, or with ice cream or whipped cream.

STUFFED ARTICHOKES

Serves 4

◆ Artichokes make an unusual individual presentation for a simple rice salad: the leaves are perfect scoops. Vary the salad with leftover vegetables or meat and your favorite vinaigrette.

4 medium artichokes, cooked,

cooled, see note

2 to 3 cups cooked rice, see Easy Rice

1 stalk celery, finely chopped

1/4 medium onion, finely chopped or

3 green onions, finely chopped

2 tablespoons fresh parsley,

finely chopped

1 medium carrot, shredded, optional

1/2 cup cooked peas, optional

1 to 2 cups cooked meat, shredded

or chopped (chicken, lamb, beef or

pork) or 1/3 pound bay shrimp

Salt and pepper, to taste

1. Mix all ingredients except artichokes. Taste and correct seasoning.

LEMON-DILL DRESSING

2 to 3 tablespoons olive oil

Zest and juice of 1 lemon (approxi-

mately 2 to 3 tablespoons juice)

1 clove garlic, pressed

1/2 teaspoon dill, or to taste

Salt and pepper, to taste

1. Mix all ingredients. Taste and adjust seasoning. Mix into rice salad. If desired, make extra dressing to serve on the side.

2. Place each artichoke on a separate serving plate. Spread the leaves open so they lie flat on the plate, exposing the small, thin inner leaves. Remove those leaves to expose the hairy choke on top of the heart.

3. With a spoon, gently remove the choke. Then equally distribute rice mixture on the heart and leaves.

NOTE: Artichokes may be microwaved, steamed or boiled but do not let them overcook so the leaves fall apart and the heart is mushy.

SEE ALSO Egg and Artichoke Burrito, and Couscous Salad.

ASPARAGUS

Serves 4

◆ Nothing is more satisfying than asparagus cooked until the stalks just begin to bend. They are perfect finger food, easy to dip into melted butter, vinaigrette, or herb-infused yogurt dip. For main courses stretch the amount of asparagus by cutting them into small pieces. Toss in a stir-fry with chicken and onions; in pasta with garlic, olive oil, and parsley; or with eggs as a frittata.

Water

Pinch salt

1 pound asparagus, cleaned and
   trimmed of fibrous bottoms

Ice cubes in a large bowl of
   cold water

METHOD 1

1. Bring water and salt to boil. Add asparagus and cook until they just begin to bend. Depending on their thickness it will take anywhere from 1 to 3 minutes.

2. Drain and immediately plunge into ice water to stop the cooking. Drain and serve or refrigerate.

METHOD 2

Microwave according to your manufacturer's instructions. Serve warm or cold.

METHOD 3

In a large saucepan, place the asparagus in about 1/2 cup water. Steam quickly on high, about 2 to 3 minutes. Serve warm.

NOTE: Method 3 is the trickiest as you must not leave the stove, for the asparagus can easily burn.

ASPARAGUS AND SHRIMP WITH BLACK BEANS

◆ This is a fast and economical meal using the stir-fry cooking technique. By cutting the food bite-size, expensive shrimp can be included along with asparagus, or any other vegetable. The pink shrimp and green asparagus make a pretty combination. Serve with rice and fruit for dessert.

1 pound fresh asparagus, trimmed
   and cut into 1-inch pieces.

1/4 to 1/2 pound shrimp, peeled,
   deveined and cut in half horizontally, or beef or chicken, cut in
   bite-size pieces

2 tablespoons salted black beans,
   chopped, see note

1 tablespoon water or white wine

2 tablespoons vegetable oil

1/2-inch piece ginger, minced

2 cloves garlic, minced

Pinch sugar

1/4 cup chicken stock

Dash sesame oil

1 teaspoon cornstarch dissolved in
   2 teaspoons water, optional

1. Mix black beans with water or wine.

2. Heat 1 tablespoon oil in skillet or wok, add black beans, ginger and garlic. Stir-fry and add chicken stock. Bring to a boil and remove contents to a bowl.

3. Heat remaining oil, add shrimp, stir-fry until almost pink. Add asparagus mixture and sesame oil to shrimp, continue to stir-fry until well mixed. Thicken with cornstarch, if desired.

NOTE: Chinese salted black beans are available in the Oriental foods section of the supermarket.

SAUTEED BANANAS

Serves 4

◆ Sauteed fruit makes a quick and easy dessert. I've used bananas here, but thinly sliced apples would also work. If you don't want to use any liquor, apple or orange juice works just fine.

1 tablespoon butter

2 to 3 tablespoons sugar, or to taste

1/4 cup rum, Cointreau, or fruit juice

Zest and juice of 1 orange

4 bananas, peeled and sliced
   lengthwise

1. In a non-stick pan, heat butter, sugar, and liquids until sugar dissolves.

2. Add bananas and cook on low to medium heat until barely soft.

Serve warm, garnished with zest, alone or with whipped cream or ice cream.

NOTE: Peaches, nectarines, or pears also work well.

WHITE BEAN PUREE

Serves 4 to 6

◆ Dried beans of any color—green, white, black—make nutritious and low-cost soups, casseroles, salads and side dishes. Leave the beans whole, or for a different texture, puree them. They can be a simple lunch with a salad and bread or part of a buffet or dinner with roasted, braised or grilled meat.

1 pound white beans

1 bay leaf

3 cloves garlic, pressed

Large pinch dried Italian

seasoning or rosemary, thyme

or oregano, or your favorite

1/2 cup white wine or water

3 to 4 cups chicken stock or water

2 tablespoons olive oil

1 clove garlic, or to taste, pressed

2 tablespoons fresh parsley, minced

Salt and pepper, to taste

1. Soak beans overnight, or alternatively, cover with water and bring to a boil. Cover pot, remove from heat and let sit about 45 minutes.

2. Drain and add all ingredients except salt, olive oil, 1 clove garlic and parsley. Simmer and cook for about 45 minutes or until beans are soft. Add more stock or water if necessary.

3. Puree in food processor, add olive oil, remaining garlic and parsley, and adjust seasoning with salt and pepper. If puree is too thick, thin with water or stock.

4. Alternatively, don't puree, add remaining ingredients and serve beans whole.

VARIATION: Black beans also work well for this dish.

WHITE BEAN AND CHICKEN CHILE

Serves 6 to 8

◆ A delicious do-ahead chile that's a change from the standard red-meat, beans and tomato variety. It's lighter in color and taste because of the chicken (or turkey) and white beans. Spice it with your favorite chile flavorings.

Serve it with homemade chips (tortillas cut and baked on cookie sheet with no oil, in 350 degree oven, about 15 minutes).

1 pound large white beans

2 large onions, chopped

4 cloves garlic, chopped

6 to 8 cups water or chicken broth

2 stalks celery, chopped

1/2 green pepper, chopped, optional

1 tablespoon chile powder, or to taste

1-1/2 teaspoons cumin, or to taste

1 teaspoon dried oregano

1/2 teaspoon dried chile flakes or

   cayenne, to taste

1 small can chopped green chiles,

   optional

2 to 3 pounds chicken or turkey

   parts, skinned, see note.

Salt and pepper, to taste

1. Soak beans in water overnight and drain. Or put beans in a large pot, cover with water, and bring to boil. Cover pot, remove from heat, and let sit about 45 minutes. Drain.

2. Add remaining ingredients, except chicken, salt and pepper, to beans and bring to a boil. Cover, reduce heat and cook about an hour or until beans begin to soften.

3. Add chicken and salt and continue cooking until chicken and beans are done.

4. Serve garnished with grated jack cheese and green onions, chopped fresh cilantro or your favorite condiments.

NOTE: It's okay to use already cooked meat, BUT add it at the last minute or it will overcook.

BLACK BEAN AND GARBANZO SALAD

Serves 4 to 6

◆ The crisp flavors of lemon and allspice make this pretty salad perfect with soup or grilled or roasted meat.

4 to 5 tablespoons olive oil

1 clove garlic, pressed

Zest and juice of 1 small lemon

1 tablespoon vinegar

1 teaspoon ground cumin

1/2 teaspoon ground allspice

2 tablespoons fresh cilantro,

chopped, optional

Pinch dried red chile pepper,

to taste, optional

Salt and pepper, to taste

2 to 2-1/2 cups cooked black beans

2 cups cooked garbanzo beans

(or 1 15-ounce can, drained)

2 stalks celery, finely chopped

1 red onion, finely chopped

or 4 green onions,

finely chopped

1. Mix all ingredients except beans, celery and onion. This is the dressing, so adjust seasonings to taste.

2. Mix remaining ingredients with dressing.

3. Serve room temperature on a bed of shredded lettuce or red cabbage for color and texture.

ASIAN STYLE MEATBALLS WITH GARLIC SAUCE

Serves 4

◆ Thai inspired, this recipe is a variation on traditional spaghetti and meatballs. Spiced with garlic and cilantro, the meatballs are tossed with noodles or rice and served with a sweet and pungent garlic sauce.

1/2 pound ground beef, pork, lamb, chicken, turkey or a combination

2 tablespoons chopped cilantro

2 cloves garlic, pressed

1 egg yolk

1/2 small onion, finely chopped

6 water chestnuts, chopped, optional

1 teaspoon fish sauce or soy sauce, to taste, optional

Black pepper, to taste

1 pound fresh Chinese noodles, cooked or 4 cups cooked rice

2 tablespoons chopped cilantro, for garnish

1. In a bowl, mix with hands all ingredients, except noodles and garnish. Shape into tiny bite-size balls. There should be about 24.

2. Saute gently in a non-stick pan until meat is no longer pink.

GARLIC SAUCE
(adapted from *Thai Home-Cooking* by William Crawford and Kamolmal Pootaraksa)

1/2 cup water

1/2 cup white vinegar

1/2 cup granulated sugar

1 teaspoon dried chile flakes or ground chile paste

4 large cloves garlic, finely chopped

Pinch salt

1. Combine all ingredients in a stainless steel pot. Bring to a boil and simmer to reduce and thicken by about a third.

2. To assemble: Place noodles or rice in a large bowl. Top with meatballs, garnish with chopped cilantro and serve sauce on the side or on top.

SPICY BEER BISCUITS

Makes 20 to 24

◆ I used to think of biscuits as difficult to make. But these zippy little gems can be made and baked in 15 minutes with ingredients already on hand. Think of them as a delicious, quick and easy last-minute addition to any meal. Try them with grilled foods, with eggs at breakfast, or with a large salad at lunch.

2 cups all-purpose flour

1 tablespoon baking powder

1/4 teaspoon salt

4 tablespoons butter

2 jalapeños, seeded and finely

   chopped or 1 teaspoon dried

   chile flakes, or to taste

1 cup beer

1. Place dry ingredients in a bowl and cut in the butter until the mixture is the consistency of coarse crumbs.

2. Add remaining ingredients and quickly mix with a fork until well blended.

3. Drop by tablespoonful onto greased baking sheet and bake in a preheated 500 degree oven for 8 to 10 minutes or until golden. Serve immediately.

NOTE: If using self-rising flour, omit baking powder and salt. If you don't have beer, use milk or buttermilk. Your biscuits will be light and tender if you work the dough quickly and gently.

BERRY CRISP

Serves 4

◆ Any fruit will work for this crisp. It's a snap to make and can be served warm, straight from the oven. It's perfect for one or two because it's made in individual dishes. Depending on diet and budget, embellish it with whipped cream or ice cream, though it's refreshing just plain. Try it with a combination of fruits, or a single fruit.

2 boxes berries, sliced if strawberries, or 4 peaches, nectarines,
   oranges, or your favorite mixture,
   peeled and sliced
2 tablespoons sugar, or to taste
2 tablespoons liqueur such as orange
   or raspberry, or orange juice
4 tablespoons butter
4 tablespoons sugar
1/2 cup flour
Pinch salt
Pinch nutmeg

1. Mix fruit with sugar and liqueur. Divide fruit equally among 4 lightly buttered individual oven-proof serving dishes such as Pyrex baking cups.

2. Place butter, sugar, flour, salt and nutmeg in a bowl and rub with hands until crumbly.

3. Sprinkle the crumbs evenly on top of each dish and bake in pre-heated 375 degree oven for about 15 or 20 minutes, or until brown and bubbly.

VARIATION: Use an 8 by 8 inch square pan and double fruit. Or, use a 9 by 13 inch baking pan and double the recipe to serve 8. Cook about 20 to 25 minutes or until brown and bubbly.

BERRY FOOL

Serves 4 to 6

◆ Fruit fools have their roots in Britain and became part of American cooking long ago. This dessert is perfect as a last-minute addition to any meal. Summer's bounty of fresh fruit—peaches, berries, figs—or cooked fruit, such as applesauce—all work well with the whipped cream.

2 tablespoons sugar, or to taste

2 cups fresh fruit, coarsely chopped

1 cup whipping cream

1 to 2 tablespoons orange or cherry
  liqueur, or to taste, or zest of 1/2
  orange or lemon, or to taste,
  optional

1. Place fruit in bowl, add sugar, mix and let sit for a few minutes. Puree. If using berries, strain to remove seeds.

2. Whip cream and fold in fruit and optional flavoring. Chill and serve.

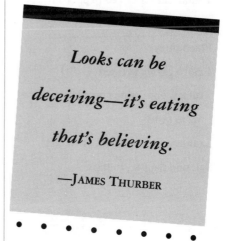

Looks can be deceiving—it's eating that's believing.

—JAMES THURBER

BLACK-EYED PEA SALAD

Serves 4

◆ In the South, black-eyed peas are eaten for good luck. These peas make an easy, no-fail salad any time of the year and are delicious with barbecued chicken and a green salad. Make the pea salad ahead for a terrific picnic dish.

1/2 pound dried black-eyed peas

1 bay leaf

3 cloves garlic, peeled and crushed

1 small bunch green onions, chopped,

   including some green tops

1 large rib celery, finely chopped

1 small carrot or red pepper for

   color, shredded or finely sliced

Pinch thyme

1 clove garlic, pressed

2 tablespoons wine vinegar,

   or to taste

3 tablespoons olive oil, or to taste

Salt and pepper, to taste

1. Put peas, bay leaf and crushed garlic into a pot, cover with water. Cover pot and boil for 2 minutes.

2. Remove from heat and let pot rest for 1 hour. Peas should not be mushy. Drain.

3. Put peas in a bowl, add the remaining ingredients. Mix well and taste to correct seasoning. Chill and serve.

BREAD SALAD

Serves 4 to 5

◆ A refreshing and slightly unusual salad that uses hearty day-old bread such as sourdough, French or Italian, as a main ingredient. It's perfect for the summer bounty of juicy tomatoes and crunchy cucumbers. Vary the proportions and add fresh herbs—basil or parsley--to taste. The simple, yet very satisfying flavors, go well with grilled meats or vegetables.

1/2 loaf day-old bread, crusts

    removed if desired, cubed, see note

1 cucumber, peeled, seeded, chopped

4 medium tomatoes, peeled, seeded,

    chopped, see note

1 small red onion, thinly sliced

1 rib celery, chopped, optional

1 green, red or yellow bell pepper,

    chopped, optional

1 teaspoon capers

4 tablespoons olive oil

2 tablespoons red wine vinegar,

    or to taste

Salt and pepper, to taste

1 tablespoon fresh parsley or basil,

    chopped, optional for garnish

1. In a large bowl, mix all ingredients and let stand at room temperature, or refrigerate at least 1 hour.

2. Mix, adjust seasonings, and if too dry add more oil and vinegar. Can also be made a day ahead.

NOTE: If bread is too hard to cut, soak it in a little water to soften. Squeeze out excess moisture before using. Simply chop the tomatoes if you don't mind the seeds. And, depending upon the juiciness of the ingredients, adjust the oil and vinegar so the bread soaks up the liquid.

HEARTY CABBAGE SOUP

Serves 4 to 6

◆ This is a hearty soup especially if made with a homemade stock. It's delicious for lunch or dinner with bread and a salad.

1 pound Kielbasa sausage, sliced

8 cups chicken or beef stock or water

1 large cabbage, cored and

  roughly chopped

1 large onion, thinly sliced

3 cloves garlic

2 stalks celery, thinly sliced

2 carrots, peeled, cut in

  small chunks

1 bay leaf

1 teaspoon mixed Italian herbs,

  to taste, optional

Salt and pepper, to taste

1. In a large pot, saute the sausage for about 2 minutes, turning frequently so it doesn't stick. Drain fat. Add water, and bring to a boil.

2. Add remaining ingredients except salt and simmer about 1 to 1-1/2 hours. Correct seasoning with salt and pepper if necessary.

I live on good soup,

not fine words.

—MOLIERE

FOURTH OF JULY SLAW

Serves 8

◆ Summer is the season for light and easy salads, and coleslaw is one of the best. Cabbage goes a long way, especially chopped, and is usually a good buy. Perfect for picnics with its cider vinegar-based dressing, this coleslaw won't spoil (as might one with a mayonnaise dressing). The presentation adds a pretty variation, though you can mix everything together for a confetti look.

1 head red cabbage, approximately

1 pound, finely chopped

1 head green cabbage, approximately

1 pound, finely chopped

1 red onion, finely chopped

1 handful fresh parsley, finely

chopped

1 small carrot, shredded, for garnish

1. Place each cabbage in a separate bowl. Divide in half the onion and parsley and add to each bowl. Mix.

2. Dress each bowl with your favorite dressing or use this one with celery seed.

CELERY SEED DRESSING

1/2 cup olive oil

1/3 cup cider vinegar, or to taste

1 heaping teaspoon celery seed

1/2 teaspoon dry mustard

Salt and pepper, to taste

1 to 2 teaspoons sugar, to taste,

optional

1. Mix all ingredients, and taste to correct seasoning. Use half of dressing for each bowl of cabbage.

2. To serve, place green cabbage in the middle of a round plate or a shallow bowl with sloping sides. Ring the outside of the green cabbage with the red, and garnish with a sprinkling of shredded carrot.

CABBAGE ROLLS

Serves 4

◆ The filling for these cabbage rolls is a whatever-you-have-on-hand filling. I use leftover rice, fresh vegetables, and season with Oriental flavors. Vary the flavors with Italian or curry spices. Or, add about 1/3 pound ground meat of your choice. The cabbage is pre-cooked (blanched, see glossary) to make it pliable.

1 head cabbage, bottom (core end)

    sliced so cabbage sits flat

2 cups (approx.) cooked rice,

    see Easy Rice

1 carrot, diced

2 stalks celery, finely sliced

1 large onion, finely chopped

For Asian style spicing:

3 green onions, finely chopped

1/2 can water chestnuts, chopped

1 piece fresh ginger, finely chopped

1 clove garlic, pressed

1 teaspoon Hoisin sauce (available in

    Oriental section of supermarket)

2 teaspoons sesame oil

Dash vinegar

Salt and pepper, to taste

Dash cayenne, optional

1 egg

Liquid for cooking: water, broth,

    wine or a mixture

1. Fill a large pot with water and bring to a boil. Put in whole cabbage and blanch, uncovered, for 5 to 7 minutes or until cabbage begins to soften. Remove cabbage and run under cold water to stop the cooking. Drain. Gently pull each leaf off the head. Pat dry.

2. In a bowl, combine remaining ingredients except liquid. Depending upon size, put 1 to 2 tablespoons filling on each cabbage leaf. Beginning at the core (thicker end) fold leaf over the filling, turning the sides up like an envelope.

3. Lay rolls seam-side-down in a skillet, add enough liquid to halfway cover them. Cover and simmer about 5 to 10 minutes. If using meat, cook at least 20 minutes.

Dip in sauce of white vinegar seasoned with grated fresh ginger.

CARROT SOUP

Serves 4 to 6

◆ Carrots are a good buy, particularly unpackaged. Those with tops on (and slightly costlier) are sweeter and better for serving as a vegetable. This soup takes minutes to prepare, and its flavors can be altered to taste. Substitute other herbs such as dill, cumin or parsley for ginger, or orange for lemon. The rice thickens the soup and makes it creamy (without the fat calories of cream).

1 tablespoon olive or vegetable oil

1 onion, thinly sliced

1-1/2 pounds carrots, scraped and
   cut into small pieces

6 to 7 cups water or chicken broth

2 tablespoons raw rice

Small piece ginger, freshly grated,
   approximately 1/2 teaspoon, or to
   taste, or 1 tablespoon chopped
   fresh parsley

Salt and pepper, to taste

Juice and zest of a lemon or orange

Pinch of curry powder, optional

1. Heat oil in a large saucepan and add onion. Saute until soft, about 2 minutes. Add carrots, water, rice, half the ginger, salt and pepper. Cover and cook until carrots are soft, about 20 minutes.

2. Puree carrot mixture in food processor or blender, adding the liquid as the mixture purees. Return to pan to heat. Before serving, add lemon juice and zest, remaining ginger and curry powder, if used. Correct seasoning.

3. To serve, top with a small dollop of sour cream or lowfat plain yogurt. Sprinkle with a bit of fresh chopped parsley (if you didn't use it in the soup) or some finely chopped green onion tops.

CELERY SALAD

Serves 4

◆ Raw celery usually appears as sticks with a dip. Here it's thinly sliced and served as a salad simply dressed with lemon juice and olive oil. The tomato adds color and texture.

8 ribs celery, thinly sliced crosswise

1 small tomato, seeded and finely
  chopped

2 tablespoons olive oil

2 tablespoons fresh lemon juice

Salt and pepper, to taste

2 tablespoons grated Parmesan
  cheese, preferably fresh

1. Put celery and tomato into a bowl.

2. In a small bowl mix oil, lemon juice, salt and pepper.

3. Toss the mixture with celery, correct seasoning.

4. To serve, top with cheese.

SEE ALSO Apple-Celery Chutney.

CHEESE BREAD

Makes 10 to 12 slices

◆ Try this easy cheese bread for breakfast, lunch or dinner. Serve it fresh from the oven or make it ahead to reheat. Add your favorite herb or leave it plain. If buttermilk isn't available, substitute regular milk mixed with lemon juice or vinegar.

3 tablespoons butter, melted
  and cooled

3 eggs or 1 egg plus 2 whites

1 cup buttermilk, or 1 cup regular
  milk mixed with 1 tablespoon
  lemon juice or vinegar and left
  for 10 minutes

2 cups flour

1 tablespoon baking powder

3/4 teaspoon baking soda

1/4 teaspoon salt

1/2 to 3/4 teaspoon dried herb
  such as rosemary, dill or
  oregano, crushed

2 cups cheddar cheese, grated

1. Grease and flour a loaf pan.

2. In a large bowl, mix butter, eggs and milk. Mix dry ingredients in a separate bowl.

3. Add flour mixture and cheese to liquid. Gently mix with a fork but don't overmix.

4. Pour into prepared pan and bake in preheated 350 degree oven for 30 to 40 minutes or until knife comes out clean when inserted into the middle of the bread.

CHICKEN LIVERS WITH APPLE AND ONION

Serves 4

◆ Versatile and economical, chicken liver is an important ingredient in dishes ranging from chopped liver and rumaki to pâtes and sautés. Loaded with vitamins and without the assertive flavor of pork and beef liver, chicken liver takes well to most herbs and spices.

Buy livers fresh. Frozen livers become grainy when cooked. The trick to cooking chicken livers is to use a medium high heat and move them quickly in the pan so they don't overcook. This dish uses an apple for additional crunch and sweetness. Serve the livers over rice or pasta.

2 to 3 tablespoons olive or
  vegetable oil
2 onions, finely sliced
1 large clove garlic, minced
1 apple, peeled, cored and
  finely diced
1 pound chicken livers, cut in
  quarters, fatty membrane trimmed

Salt and pepper, to taste
1 teaspoon Italian herb seasoning
  or your favorite such as oregano,
  basil, thyme, to taste
2 to 3 tablespoons red wine
2 tablespoons fresh parsley,
  finely chopped

1. Heat 1 tablespoon oil in large skillet. Saute onions and garlic until soft. Add apple and continue cooking until apple begins to soften. Remove mixture to a bowl.

2. Add remaining oil to skillet and place on medium high heat. Add livers, salt, pepper and herbs, and saute mixture until livers are barely pink, about 2 minutes.

3. Add onion mixture and wine to the livers, toss to mix the flavors. Taste to correct seasoning.

4. Serve on a bed of rice and top with chopped parsley.

SAUTEED CHICKEN LIVERS WITH PASTA

Serves 4

◆ Easy to prepare, the livers cook while the pasta boils. Chicken livers are common in Italian cuisine, simply cooked with uncomplicated seasonings. Toss the livers with the pasta or serve each separately.

1/2 cup flour, approximately

Salt and pepper, to taste

1 pound chicken livers, rinsed, fatty
   membrane trimmed, separated
   and patted dry

2 to 3 tablespoons olive oil

2 tablespoons walnut or olive oil

2 tablespoons red wine vinegar

2 tablespoons port, red or white wine

3 to 4 tablespoons mixed fresh herbs
   such as basil, oregano, chives and
   thyme or any one alone, or
   1 tablespoon dried herbs

2 to 3 tablespoons walnuts, chopped

1 pound fettuccine, cooked and
   lightly tossed with olive oil
   and fresh pepper

1. Mix flour with salt and pepper, and lightly dredge livers. Heat the 3 tablespoons oil in a large skillet and gently saute livers on medium high heat until they are pink inside, about 3 minutes.

2. While livers are cooking, put walnut, red wine vinegar and port with half the fresh herbs (or all the dried) in a small saucepan and boil about 1 minute. Add sauce to livers and cook until livers are no longer pink inside, about 3 to 5 minutes.

3. Serve livers separately, tossed with remaining fresh herbs and walnuts. Or, toss with pasta and garnish with walnuts.

WARM CHICKEN SALAD WITH MUSTARD VINAIGRETTE

Serves 4

◆ This colorful salad is a low-cost meal-in-one because it uses less meat and more greens. It's a counterpoint of cold and warm, crunchy and soft, flexible in its composition, (see Variations) and easy to prepare. It makes a delicious lunch or light summer dinner. Cook the chicken in a non-stick skillet to cut fat and calories.

1 head lettuce such as red or green

   leaf, romaine or a combination,

   ripped into bite-size pieces

1 carrot, shredded

1 bunch radishes, quartered

1/2 pound, (approx.) chicken

   parts, see note

1. In a large bowl, combine everything but the chicken, and refrigerate.

2. In a non-stick skillet, saute the chicken until done. Remove skin and bone and cut into small pieces. Lay warm chicken over the greens and top with mustard vinaigrette.

MUSTARD VINAIGRETTE

5 tablespoons olive oil

2 to 3 tablespoons wine vinegar,

   lemon juice, or to taste

1 teaspoon Dijon mustard,

   or to taste

1 clove garlic, pressed

Salt and pepper, to taste

Mix all ingredients and pour over salad. Toss and serve.

VARIATIONS: Substitute cooked and flaked fish such as salmon or snapper, or beef, lamb or pork. Use your favorite dressing and vary the salad ingredients to preference.

NOTE: It's possible to use whole wings or legs, and serve with bone in. Or use boned meat.

ORANGE CHICKEN

Serves 4 to 6

◆ Easy and versatile, this chicken dish is great for tacos, burritos and salads. To get the most from your shopping dollar, use legs and thighs or a whole chicken. Four pounds of boned meat will easily serve 5 or 6, especially when mixed with beans, rice, lettuce, chips or tortillas.

3 to 4 pounds chicken or turkey,

bone and skin on

1 medium onion, quartered

1/2 bay leaf

1/2 teaspoon ground cumin

Water to cover chicken

1-1/2 to 2 cups orange juice

1/2 teaspoon dried chile flakes

1/2 teaspoon oregano

1/2 teaspoon cumin

1/2 red onion, thinly sliced

2 tablespoons cilantro, chopped

Salt and pepper, to taste

1. In a large pot put hicken, onion, bay leaf, cumin, and enough water to cover the chicken. Bring to a boil and immediately turn down to simmer. Skim, cover and simmer about 20 minutes. Remove from heat and let pot rest, covered, for about 40 minutes. Place meat in a bowl to cool.

2. When cool, remove skin and bones. Shred and put into a bowl.

3. Add remaining ingredients, mix and correct seasoning.

4. Chill overnight. Serve as a salad with lettuce and chips, or warm with rice or beans in a burrito.

ROAST CHICKEN

Serves 4

◆ Roast chicken is one of the most satisfying dishes to eat. It's also easy to make.

1 whole fryer, at least 3 pounds

Salt and pepper, to taste

**1 whole orange or lemon, pricked
    with a fork**

1/4 onion

Small handful fresh parsley, optional

1. Remove giblets and liver from chicken cavity. Rub cavity and skin with salt and pepper as desired. Place orange, onion and parsley (if used) in cavity.

2. Roast breast-side-down in a pre-heated 375 degree oven for 40 to 50 minutes, or until juices run clear when leg joint is pricked with a fork. If a crisp skin is desired, turn chicken breast up halfway through cooking.

NOTE: For a quick chutney to serve with the chicken, remove orange, parsley and onion and process in a

food processor with some of the pan juices for flavor. Or make a simple gravy with the pan juices.

PAN GRAVY

1. Pour juices into a large measuring cup or bowl. Skim off fat.

2. Return liquid to roasting pan and place over medium high heat. Scrape up bits of brown on bottom and cook until reduced by one-half.

MUSHROOM GRAVY

2 tablespoons degreased pan drippings

1/2 pound mushrooms, thinly sliced

**1 to 1-1/2 cups water, chicken stock,
    wine, or a mixture**

Salt and pepper, to taste

Use the chicken pan for the sauce. Pour off grease; leave about 2 tablespoons of drippings. Add water to loosen the bits off bottom. Add mushrooms and cook for 8 to 10 minutes, medium heat. Correct seasoning with salt and pepper.

CRUNCHY CHICKEN SALAD WITH SNOW

Serves 4

◆ This variation of a chicken salad makes use of dried rice sticks available in Asian markets and some supermarkets. When cooked, rice sticks can also be used in stir-fry dishes for a crunchy texture and a snowy white garnish. Be sure the oil is hot, so the rice sticks puff up immediately. Use leftover beef or pork in place of the chicken.

1 to 2 cups vegetable oil

   for deep frying

1 handful dried rice sticks

1 head lettuce, coarsely chopped

1 large cucumber, peeled, seeded

   and cut into 1/2-inch slices

5 green onions, finely chopped

1 cup bean sprouts

1 large carrot, finely shredded

3 cups cooked chicken,

   pork or beef

1/2 cup chopped peanuts, optional

1/4 cup chopped cilantro, optional

1. Heat oil in a skillet or wok to 350 or 375 degrees on deep-fry thermometer. Crush rice sticks in your hand before adding to oil. Stir-fry for 1 second. When puffed, remove from heat immediately and place on a paper towel-lined plate to drain and cool.

2. Arrange lettuce on a platter. In a large bowl, mix rest of ingredients with dressing and lay over the lettuce. Garnish with rice sticks.

SESAME DRESSING

1 clove garlic, pressed

1/2-inch fresh ginger, peeled

   and minced

2 tablespoons sesame oil

6 tablespoons white vinegar

Pinch sugar

Dash soy sauce, to taste, optional

Black pepper, to taste

1/2 teaspoon dried chile flakes,

   to taste, optional

Blend all ingredients and toss with salad.

CHINESE CHICKEN SALAD

Serves 4 to 6

◆ A favorite at Paragary's Bar and Oven in Sacramento, this is an easy summer salad. Everything is prepared ahead of time and tossed just before serving to avoid sogginess. Salted black beans are available in the Oriental section of the supermarket.

1 medium napa cabbage, chopped
   in 3/8-inch strips, about 8 cups

3 pounds chicken parts, cooked,
   skinned, boned, shredded,
   or 2 breasts, see note

1/3 cup whole cashews

1 bunch green onions, finely
   chopped for garnish

1. Place cabbage and chicken in a large bowl.

2. Roast cashews in preheated 300 degree oven for 15 minutes. Cool and add to chicken and cabbage.

BLACK BEAN DRESSING

2 teaspoons minced garlic

2 teaspoons minced ginger

1 tablespoon salted black beans

1/4 cup rice vinegar

1/4 cup light soy sauce

1 tablespoon sesame oil

1 tablespoon sugar

1 tablespoon Dijon mustard

1/2 cup peanut or light olive oil

1. Put ginger, garlic and black beans in processor. Process.

2. Add remaining ingredients except oil. With motor running, add oil slowly.

3. Toss with chicken mixture and garnish with scallions.

NOTE: To poach whole chicken: Put chicken with 2 green onions and a piece of ginger in a pot and cover with water. Bring to a boil, immediately turn to simmer. Skim. Cover and simmer for 20 minutes. Remove from heat and let chicken rest in liquid, about 40 minutes.

CHICKEN WITH RED WINE

Serves 8, 2 pieces each

◆ Perfect for a party on a cold winter night, this dish can be made ahead. Serve it with rice or cornmeal (polenta), a salad and dessert.

4 tablespoons flour

Salt and pepper, to taste

2 whole fryers, cut up into 8 serving

pieces, reserving the necks, backs

and gizzards for broth, see note.

1/4 pound salt pork or bacon, cut in

small pieces and blanched

4 tablespoons olive oil

16 small mushrooms, halved, or

about 1/2 pound mushrooms

2 onions, cut in eighths lengthwise

2 stalks celery, chopped, 1-inch pieces

2 carrots, chopped, 1-inch pieces

4 - 6 cloves garlic, minced or pressed

1 bay leaf

1/2 teaspoon thyme, or to taste

1 /2 teaspoon tarragon, or to taste

Large pinch rosemary, or to taste

1 bottle red wine such as Burgundy,

Cabernet Sauvignon or Zinfandel

1. Mix flour with salt and pepper and dredge chicken pieces.

2. Heat large skillet and saute the salt pork or bacon until almost crisp. Remove meat from skillet, leaving the rendered fat.

3. Add 2 tablespoons olive oil and on medium high heat, brown the chicken pieces in small batches. Remove pieces as they brown on the outside, but do not cook through.

4. If necessary, add the remaining olive oil and saute the vegetables until just soft. Remove vegetables and drain fat.

5. Add chicken, vegetables, herbs and wine to a large casserole or pot. Cover and simmer for 25 or 30 minutes or bake in preheated 375 degree oven about 35 minutes until chicken is tender.

NOTE: To cut the fat during cooking, skin the chicken first. Dish can be made ahead and reheated. Skim any fat before reheating.

EASY BUFFALO CHICKEN

Serves 4 to 6

◆ Buffalo chicken wings, made famous in Buffalo, New York, are a cinch to make at home. Here these usually deep-fried, spicy wings are baked, sauced, and served with the traditional celery sticks and a lowfat blue cheese dressing made with yogurt and mayonnaise (rather than mayonnaise and sour cream).

24 chicken wings, or 3 to 4 pounds
   chicken parts such as legs and
   thighs, or 1 whole fryer cut up
Salt and pepper, to taste
4 to 5 tablespoons butter, olive or
   vegetable oil or mixture
1 tablespoon white vinegar
1 to 5 tablespoons Tabasco or
   Louisiana hot sauce, to taste

1. Rub salt and pepper on the wings or under the skin of the parts. Bake in preheated 450 degree oven for 20 to 25 minutes, until skin is crisp and meat just pulls away from bone.

2. In a saucepan heat remaining ingredients.

3. To serve: Lay chicken on a platter and pour sauce over, or serve sauce separately so guests can control degree of hotness.

BLUE CHEESE DRESSING
(for celery sticks)

3/4 cup mayonnaise, preferably
   lowfat
3/4 cup non- or lowfat yogurt
   or light sour cream
1 small clove garlic, pressed
2 tablespoons onion, finely chopped
4 tablespoons fresh parsley,
   finely chopped
2 to 3 tablespoons blue cheese,
   crumbled, or to taste
1 tablespoon white vinegar
1 tablespoon lemon juice
Black pepper, to taste
Cayenne pepper, to taste

1. In a bowl, mix all ingredients. Chill and serve with celery sticks and Buffalo Chicken.

SPICY CHICKEN

Serves 4

◆ The seductive flavors of cinnamon and cumin, along with lots of onions, give this chicken an exotic taste found in Indian and Moroccan dishes. Serve it with rice or potatoes or a hearty bread to sop up the sauce.

1 fryer, skinned and cut into

    8 pieces, use backs and necks

    for chicken stock

8 ounces nonfat unflavored yogurt

1/2 teaspoon ground cumin,

    or to taste

1/4 teaspoon ground cinnamon,

    or to taste

2 cloves garlic, pressed

1 to 2 tablespoons vegetable

    or olive oil

3 medium onions, thinly sliced

1 small bay leaf

1 15-ounce can chopped tomatoes

Pinch sugar

Salt and pepper, to taste

1/4 teaspoon dried chile flakes,

    or to taste

2 tablespoons fresh cilantro or

    parsley, finely chopped

1. Put chicken in a large bowl and mix well with yogurt, cumin, cinnamon and garlic. Marinate at least 2 hours or overnight in the refrigerator.

2. Heat the oil in a large skillet, then add onions and saute until golden. Add chicken and marinade and cook until pieces begin to brown.

3. Add bay leaf, tomatoes, sugar, salt, pepper and chile flakes, mix, cover and simmer for about 20 minutes or until chicken is done. Mix in 1 tablespoon parsley or cilantro. Taste to correct seasoning. Can be made ahead and reheated.

4. To serve, garnish with remaining parsley or cilantro.

SIMPLE CHICKEN STOCK

Makes about 10 cups

◆ A good stock makes a good soup. For economy, use chicken backs and wings or a whole chicken (the thighs and breast can be used for salads and stir-fry). Add an onion, carrot and celery for a more flavorful broth. Use beef knuckle bones for beef stock and roast the bones first to give a deeper color to the liquid. A pressure cooker cuts the cooking time considerably.

3 pounds chicken backs and

necks or 1 whole fryer

12 cups water

1. Put water and chicken in a large pot. Bring to a boil. Skim the top and then let it simmer for 3 to 4 hours.

2. Cool and strain.

3. Can be frozen in small portions such as ice cube size or 1 cup servings.

CHOCOLATE ANGEL FOOD CAKE

Serves 8 to 10

◆ Angel food cake is a favorite dessert of mine because it has no fat, is low in calories, and can be dressed up with fresh summer fruits such as strawberries or peaches.

1 cup sifted cake flour

1/4 cup unsweetened cocoa

1-1/2 cups sugar

12 large egg whites, approximately

   1-1/2 cups, at room temperature

1-1/2 teaspoons cream of tartar

Pinch salt

1-3/4 teaspoons vanilla or

   almond extract

1. Sift flour, cocoa and 3/4 cup sugar together four times.

2. In a large mixing bowl combine remaining ingredients, except for sugar. Beat at high speed with an electric mixer until whites are in soft peaks. Gradually add remaining 3/4 cup sugar and beat until stiff peaks are formed.

3. Sift 1/4 of flour mixture over egg whites and fold into batter, about 15 strokes. Repeat with remaining flour, 1/3 at a time.

4. Pour mixture into an ungreased 10-inch tube pan. Run a knife through the mixture to get rid of air bubbles. Bake in preheated 375 degree oven 30 to 35 minutes.

5. To set the cake, invert pan and cool for at least 1-1/2 hours. When cool, run a knife around the edges to loosen and remove from pan.

NOTE: Be sure egg whites are room temperature and in a clean dry bowl. They won't whip if they contain any egg yolk or other fat, water or eggshell. Do not fold flour mixture with electric beater. Use a spatula. Don't overfold because this deflates the whites. The cooked cake softens when exposed to air.

VARIATION: For a white angel food cake, substitute 1/4 cup flour for the cocoa.

CHOCOLATE DIPPED FIGS

Serves 6 to 8

◆ Alone, these are a tasty ending to any meal. They are a cinch to make ahead and are great kept on hand for a quick snack.

1 8-ounce package dried figs

1/2 cup semi-sweet chocolate chips

1. Melt chocolate in microwave or on low heat in a saucepan.

2. Holding stem, dip fig in chocolate. Place on waxed paper. Repeat for each fig.

3. Refrigerate to set the chocolate.

These work well as garnish for Pumpkin Custard.

We never repent of having eaten too little.

—THOMAS JEFFERSON

EASY CHOCOLATE TRUFFLES

Makes 24 small truffles

◆Homemade truffles are easy to do ahead of time and keep well in the freezer. They may be flavored with Grand Marnier or coffee. I prefer to make them small, because one or two are enough to satisfy any chocoholic.

1 cup (6 ounces) semi-sweet

chocolate chips

4 tablespoons cream

1 teaspoon instant coffee, dissolved

in 1 tablespoon warm water,

or 2 tablespoons liqueur

2 tablespoons unsalted butter

1 to 2 tablespoons unsweetened

cocoa

1. In a saucepan, melt chocolate with cream, flavoring and butter on low heat. Mix well. Or heat in microwave according to manufacturer's instructions.

2. Place in a bowl, tightly cover and refrigerate until firm.

3. Put cocoa in a shallow bowl. Place bowl of truffle mixture in a bowl of ice.

4. With a teaspoon or small melon baller, take about 1/2 teaspoon of chocolate mixture. With butter-greased hands, quickly form chocolate into a marble-size ball and roll in cocoa to completely coat. Place on waxed paper and refrigerate. Continue until all mixture is used.

ORANGE-CHOCOLATE SAUCE

Serves 4

◆ This easy sauce was adapted from one originated by Dolores Cakebread at Cakebread Cellars, a winery in the Napa Valley. Use it over fruit, ice cream, or angel food cake. There is no added sugar or butter so it's low in calories and fat.

4 ounces semi-sweet chocolate

  (approximately 3/4 cup of

  chocolate chips)

1/2 cup orange juice, or hearty

  red wine such as

  Cabernet Sauvignon

Zest of 1/2 orange, minced,

  optional

1. Put ingredients into micro-waveable dish.

2. Cover with plastic wrap and microwave for 30 to 45 seconds on high or long enough to melt the chocolate. Or place all ingredients in a saucepan over low heat.

3. Stir until well mixed.

CORN-RAISIN CHUTNEY

Serves 4

◆ Here's a zesty raisin relish
that includes fresh summer corn,
although frozen can be used. Make
it ahead; it won't spoil on a picnic.
Use the relish as a delicious side
dish with grilled chicken, or as a
dressing for a cold salad such as
greens or plain boiled potatoes.

1 ear fresh corn, kernels removed,

   or approximately 1 cup

   frozen corn

1 cup raisins

1/2 cup cider vinegar

1/2 small onion, finely chopped

1 small slice fresh ginger,

   finely chopped

1/4 small green or red pepper,

   chopped, optional

2 tablespoons sugar

1 teaspoon mustard seeds

1 teaspoon dry mustard

Dash salt

Dash red pepper flakes

1. Put all ingredients in a saucepan.
Bring to a boil.

2. Cover and simmer for 10 to 15
minutes.

3. Cool and serve.

SEE ALSO Apple-Celery Chutney.

CORN AND BROCCOLI SALAD

Serves 4

◆ The proportions aren't too important here—use however much you have of leftover fresh corn. When fresh corn isn't available, frozen will work or try it with cauliflower. Shredded carrot adds color. Cook the dressing ingredients to meld the flavors and cut the harshness of raw garlic. Lemon juice gives it a fresh finish.

1 pound broccoli, cut into

    bite-size pieces

2 ears cooked fresh corn, kernels

    removed, or approximately 2 cups

    cooked frozen corn

1 carrot, grated, optional

1. Steam, boil or microwave broccoli until slightly crunchy. Cool.

2. Combine all ingredients in a bowl.

SPICY LEMON DRESSING

4 tablespoons olive oil

1 clove garlic, pressed

1 to 2 tablespoons fresh parsley,

    chopped

1/4 to 1/2 teaspoon dried chile flakes

1/2 teaspoon anchovy paste, or

    to taste, optional

2 tablespoons lemon juice, or to taste

Fresh pepper, to taste

1. In a saucepan, heat oil, garlic, parsley, chile flakes and anchovy paste. Stir until the ingredients begin to soften, about 30 seconds, or until the oil just begins to bubble around the edges of the pan.

2. Let cool slightly and add lemon juice and pepper. Adjust seasoning.

3. Toss with salad and serve chilled or room temperature.

CORNMEAL (POLENTA) WITH HERBS

Serves 4 to 6

◆ Cornmeal (polenta) makes an easy side dish or appetizer. The trick to smooth polenta is to *slowly* add the cornmeal to the boiling water while stirring constantly. Serve warm. Look for polenta in the bulk foods section of the supermarket. It's perfect with Chicken in Red Wine or grilled or roasted meats and poultry.

1 tablespoon olive oil

1 onion, chopped

6 cups water or chicken stock

4 tablespoons parsley, chopped

1 tablespoon dried Italian herb

   seasoning

1 teaspoon salt

Black pepper, to taste

2 cups coarse-ground cornmeal

8 tablespoons grated cheddar or

   Parmesan cheese, optional

1. In a large pot, heat olive oil and saute onion until it softens.

2. Add liquid and bring to a boil. Turn heat to simmer and add seasonings. Slowly, in a thin stream, add the cornmeal. Stir constantly until thick, and cornmeal pulls away from sides of pan, about 20 minutes.

3. Pour into a greased jelly-roll pan (11 by 15 inches) and spread evenly. Sprinkle with cheese, if desired. Let it rest for 15 minutes.

4. Cut into squares, diamonds, or cookie cutter shapes. Serve warm. Can be made ahead and reheated under a broiler. Alternatively, use a loaf pan in place of the jelly-roll pan and slice the loaf.

GREEN ONION-CORNMEAL PANCAKES

Makes about 18

◆ These easy and economical green onion-cornmeal pancakes are adapted from *Biscuits, Spoonbread, and Sweet Potato Pie* by Bill Neal. They are delicious with grilled meats or poultry.

1 cup cornmeal

1/2 cup flour

1/4 teaspoon salt

1 teaspoon sugar

2 teaspoons baking powder

1/2 teaspoon baking soda

2 eggs

1-1/4 cups buttermilk

2 tablespoons melted butter

2/3 cup finely chopped
   green onions

1. Sift dry ingredients together.

2. Beat eggs with a fork and add buttermilk and butter. Add to dry ingredients and mix to make a smooth batter. Fold in green onions. Let stand 10 minutes.

3. Drop by tablespoonfuls onto large, lightly greased skillet. Cook on medium heat until bubbles form. Turn pancakes and brown on other side.

NOTE: These pancakes are terrific for breakfast. Increase the sugar to 2 tablespoons and omit the green onions.

CORNMEAL-GINGER PANCAKES

Serves 4

◆ Powdered or fresh ginger adds an elusive and subtle flavor while the addition of cornmeal gives a slightly crunchy texture. These pancakes are easy to make and delicious with a fresh fruit compote or applesauce.

1/3 cup cornmeal

2/3 cup flour

2 tablespoons sugar

1 teaspoon baking powder

1/2 teaspoon powdered ginger or

3/4 teaspoon finely grated

fresh ginger

1/2 teaspoon ground allspice or

combination of ground cinnamon,

clove and nutmeg, to taste,

optional

Pinch salt

1 cup lowfat milk

1 egg

2 tablespoons vegetable oil

1. Combine dry ingredients in a bowl. Mix in milk, egg and oil.

2. Drop by tablespoonfuls onto non-stick pan.

3. Cook on medium heat until bubbles form. Turn pancakes and brown on other side.

COUSCOUS SALAD

Serves 4 to 6

◆ The Moroccan pasta called couscous is a precooked dry semolina fine grain cereal. Make this warm-weather salad a day ahead. A box of couscous will make at least two large meals and it costs about $1.35. Vary the vegetables according to preference and seasonal availability, and add any leftover roasted meat for a heartier meal.

4 cups water or chicken broth

1/2 teaspoon turmeric, for color,

   optional

1/2 teaspoon cinnamon

2 tablespoons olive oil

2 cloves garlic, pressed

1/2 teaspoon ground ginger or

   1 teaspoon fresh ginger, minced

2 cups couscous

1 onion, finely chopped

2 medium zucchini, chopped

1 carrot, shredded

1/2 cup raisins

2 tablespoons fresh parsley,

   finely chopped

Zest and juice of 1 lemon, or to taste

2 to 3 tablespoons olive oil

Salt and pepper, to taste

1/2 cup almonds, toasted and chopped

1. In a large pot bring to a boil water or broth, turmeric, cinnamon, olive oil, garlic and ginger.

2. Add couscous, stir, cover and remove from heat. Let stand about 10 minutes while the couscous absorbs the liquid. Add onion, zucchini, carrot, and raisins. Mix and cover while the mixture cools slightly, about 10 minutes.

3. Mix parsley, lemon zest, lemon juice, and olive oil and pour over couscous. Mix, cover and refrigerate at least overnight.

4. To serve, let salad come to room temperature and adjust seasonings. Top with almonds.

VARIATIONS: Delete vegetables, flavor with Italian seasonings and use to stuff artichokes, tomatoes or green peppers.

CRANBERRY SALAD

Serves 6 to 8

◆ Most often found in a can, cranberries are an easy side dish for roasted or grilled meats. This quick, delicious and colorful salad uses fresh cranberries. It works well with turkey, other poultry, and roast pork.

2 oranges, 1 peeled, seeded and diced, the other finely chopped including peel

2 green apples, cored and chopped

1 papaya, peeled, seeded and diced, optional

1 12-ounce package fresh cranberries, chopped

1/3 to 1/2 cup sugar, or to taste

1-1/2 cups walnuts, chopped, optional

1-1/2 tablespoons fresh parsley, finely chopped

1. Place all ingredients, except walnuts and parsley, in a large bowl.

2. Cover and refrigerate at least 8 hours.

3. To serve, mix in walnuts and sprinkle chopped parsley on top.

COOL CUCUMBER SALAD

Serves 4

◆ This refreshing and healthful salad is frequently served as a cooling contrast to spicy Indian food. It's a cinch to make and is perfect with grilled meats. Use bananas or potatoes instead of cucumber, or add a pinch of hot ground pepper or mint and adjust seasonings to personal taste.

1 medium cucumber, peeled, seeded
and coarsely grated, squeezed
to remove liquid
1 tablespoon onion, finely chopped,
optional
1 small tomato, finely diced, optional
1 cup plain lowfat yogurt, or 3/4 cup
yogurt and 1/4 cup lowfat
sour cream
1/2 teaspoon salt, or to taste
1 teaspoon ground cumin, roasted,
see note
1 tablespoon fresh cilantro,
chopped

1. Mix all ingredients together. Adjust seasoning.

2. Chill covered for at least 1 hour.

NOTE: Roast cumin in a small ungreased skillet on low heat for about 30 seconds or until it gives off a slight aroma of cumin.

EGG AND ARTICHOKE BURRITOS

Serves 4

◆ This unusual lowfat meatless burrito combines eggs with artichoke hearts packed in water, salsa, onions, a little cheese, and leftover rice. It's perfect with a salad.

1 tablespoon olive or vegetable oil

1 onion, chopped

1 rib celery, chopped

1 large clove garlic, pressed

1/2 of 14-ounce jar of artichoke

  hearts in water, drained,

  coarsely chopped

1/2 cup salsa, or to taste

1 cup leftover cooked rice, optional

8 large eggs, beaten, or use 4 yolks

  and 8 whites

Salt and pepper, to taste

4 tablespoons cheddar, jack or

  Parmesan cheese, grated

4 large flour tortillas, warmed

1. In a non-stick pan, heat oil and saute onion, celery and garlic until soft.

2. Add artichoke hearts, salsa and rice. Saute 1 minute.

3. Add eggs, scramble and cook to desired doneness. Adjust seasoning. Remove from heat.

4. Divide mixture equally on each tortilla, top with cheese, and fold like an envelope. Serve with additional salsa if desired.

EGG DROP SOUP

Serves 4

◆ A simple and satisfying soup. Vary it by adding thinly sliced vegetables or leftover shredded meat.

4 cups chicken stock

1/2-inch piece fresh ginger,

  crushed, optional

1 egg, beaten with a fork,

  no froth

Salt and pepper, to taste

2 tablespoons green onion,

  finely chopped

1. In a pot, bring stock and ginger (if used) to a boil.

2. Turn off heat, and in a slow, thin stream add the egg, stirring constantly. The egg will form threads in the broth.

3. Taste to correct seasoning.

4. Serve garnished with chopped green onion.

Of soup and love, the first is best.

—Spanish Proverb

ALMOND MERINGUE PIE WITH CHOCOLATE SAUCE

Serves 8

◆ Whip up this lowfat, no choles-terol, feather-light meringue pie with just four egg whites and a lit-tle chocolate. Use an electric beat-er, if possible, to beat egg whites.

4 large egg whites, see note

1/4 teaspoon cream of tartar

Scant 1/4 teaspoon almond extract

1/2 cup sugar

1/4 cup unsalted toasted almonds,
   chopped

1/2 cup semi-sweet chocolate,
   1/4 cup of it chopped, chips work
   well

Juice of half orange, optional

1. Beat egg whites until frothy. Add cream of tartar and continue beating to form soft peaks. While beating, add almond extract and slowly add sugar, beating until stiff peaks form.

2. Fold in almonds and 1/4 cup chopped chocolate. Put meringue in a 9-inch pie pan lined with parch-ment paper or Von Snedaker's Magic Baking Sheet (see note). Bake in preheated 300 degree oven for 1 hour and 15 minutes, or until top is firm and a knife comes out clean from the center. Center will be soft.

3. Remove and cool. Serve with chocolate sauce made from re-maining 1/4 cup chocolate melted with orange juice.

NOTE: Be sure egg whites are room temperature and in a clean, dry bowl. They won't whip if they contain egg yolk, other fat, water or eggshell.

Meringue softens when there is any moisture in the air. Keep well covered before serving.

Von Snedaker's reusable Magic Baking Sheets, 12021 Wilshire Boulevard, Suite 231, Los Angeles, California 90025, telephone (213) 395-6365.

ALMOST SOUFFLE

Serves 4

◆ Let the kids make this easy breakfast dish. It puffs up in the oven, though not as high as a souffle, and then deflates once it begins to cool. Serve it straight from the pan at the table. Make the basic recipe to serve with yogurt, sour cream, fruit, syrup, or powdered sugar. Or make it with herbs and cheese for a heartier version.

4 eggs

2/3 cup milk

2/3 cup flour

1 teaspoon vanilla

3 tablespoons butter

1. In a blender or with a fork, beat eggs. Add milk, continue beating, add flour and vanilla and beat until frothy.

2. In preheated 425 degree oven, melt butter in an 8-inch cast-iron skillet or any two-quart ovenproof dish not more than 3 inches deep.

3. With a hot pad, remove pan, swirl butter around edges and quickly add the egg mixture. Cook for 20 to 25 minutes.

4. Remove and serve immediately.

SAVORY VARIATION: Omit the vanilla and add 1 clove pressed garlic; 2 tablespoons chopped, fresh parsley; and 1/2 teaspoon oregano. To serve, sprinkle with a heaping tablespoon of grated cheese such as Parmesan or cheddar.

CRUNCHY FILO PIZZA

Serves 6

◆ Look for the paper-thin filo sheets sold boxed, by the pound, either fresh or frozen. One pound has about 24 sheets and will make three large pizzas. The topping is your choice, though I like thinly sliced zucchini, tomatoes and even black olives. Topped with cheese it becomes richer, and costlier. Cut it into small pieces for a delicious appetizer or serve as part of a light lunch or dinner.

4 tablespoons olive oil

1 clove garlic, pressed

7 sheets filo dough (approximately

12 x 15 inches)

1/2 cup Parmesan cheese, grated

1 cup mozzarella, grated, optional

1 small red onion, thinly sliced

1 small green zucchini, thinly sliced

1 small yellow zucchini, thinly sliced

2 medium tomatoes, thinly sliced

1 to 2 tablespoons mixed fresh

herbs such as basil, thyme, or

oregano, finely chopped or

1 tablespoon dried

Handful of black olives, optional

Salt and pepper, to taste

1. Brush lightly with olive oil a baking sheet large enough for the filo sheets. Add garlic to remaining olive oil.

2. Lay a sheet of filo on the baking sheet, lightly brush it with olive oil and sprinkle with about 1 tablespoon Parmesan. Lay the next sheet over it and repeat the process with the remaining sheets. On the top sheet sprinkle mozzarella if used.

3. Quickly toss zucchini in any remaining olive oil and lay vegetables on top. Sprinkle with herbs, salt, pepper, and remaining Parmesan cheese.

4. Bake in preheated 375 degree oven for 15 to 25 minutes, or until edges are golden and cheese is melted.

5. Cut into squares and serve warm or at room temperature.

SEE ALSO Filo Kisses.

FILO KISSES

Makes 100

◆ Filo, those paper-thin sheets of pastry, make a crunchy wrapping for just about any filling. Teamed here with fresh spinach and cheese, they make tasty appetizers. Or, cut the sheets larger and serve as the entree for a vegetarian meal. Make ahead of time and freeze.

2 bunches fresh spinach, stemmed

    and steamed or 2 packages frozen,

    thawed and drained

8 ounces mozzarella, grated

4 tablespoons Parmesan cheese,

    grated, optional

1/2 to 3/4 teaspoon freshly grated

    nutmeg, or to taste

Black pepper, to taste

8 sheets filo dough

1 to 2 cubes butter, melted

1. Cool spinach and squeeze out moisture by hand or in a tea towel. Chop it finely. Put in a bowl with cheeses, nutmeg and pepper and mix.

2. Working quickly so filo doesn't dry, take 1 sheet filo and brush with butter, then add another sheet and brush with butter. Cut sheet into 24 squares (5 cuts on the long edge; 3 cuts on the short edge).

3. Put a tiny bit of spinach mixture in center of each square and close by pinching the dough and gently twisting to make a kiss. Repeat procedure with remaining filo sheets. Can be frozen at this point.

4. Bake on an ungreased baking sheet in preheated 350 degree oven for 8 to 10 minutes or until golden. If using frozen kisses, do not defrost before cooking. Makes about 100.

NOTE: Have filling ready before working with the dough. While working, keep the sheets covered to prevent them from drying out.

SEE ALSO Filo Pizza.

SIMPLE FISH

Serves 4

◆ Fresh snapper is readily available and easy to cook, though any firm-fleshed fish will work. The fillets can be poached in water, orange juice, wine or a combination. Since the fish simmers in the herb-infused liquid with no oil or fat, it remains low in calories, yet high in flavor. The cost of fish may seem high, but with little or no waste it is a good value. Complete the meal with a salad and fruit.

1 cup water or wine

1 stalk celery, finely diced

1 bay leaf

1/2 onion, finely sliced

1 clove garlic, pressed

Salt and pepper, to taste

1/2 teaspoon dill, oregano, rosemary
   or your favorite herb

1 pound snapper or other firm fish

2 carrots, finely shredded

2 tablespoons parsley,
   finely chopped

1. In a pan large enough for the fish, put water or wine, celery, bay leaf, onion, garlic, salt, pepper, and herbs. Bring to a boil, then turn to simmer.

2. Add fish, cover and cook until fish turns opaque and flakes easily, about 3 to 5 minutes, depending on the thickness of the fish.

3. Alternatively, cook in microwave oven according to manufacturer's instructions, approximately 2 to 3 minutes on high...fish is done when it just flakes.

4. To serve, make a bed of carrots, place fish on top and garnish with chopped parsley.

FISH WITH SWEET AND SOUR SAUCE

Serves 4

◆ Use this sweet and sour sauce with your favorite roasted meat, turkey, chicken, shrimp, or meatloaf. For a fast and tasty dish, I paired it with red snapper cooked in the microwave. Along with rice and a salad, this makes a delicious lowfat meal.

1/2 onion, sliced

1 carrot, sliced in thin 2-inch strips

1 stalk celery, sliced in thin
    2-inch strips

1 pound snapper fillets

6 snow peas, thinly sliced lengthwise

Salt and pepper, to taste

1. Lay vegetables, except snow peas, on a microwaveable dish. Put fish on top, sprinkle snow peas on fish. Season, cover and microwave on high for 4 to 5 minutes.

2. Pour off liquid.

SWEET AND SOUR SAUCE

1/2 cup water

1/2 cup sugar

1/2 cup white vinegar

16-ounce can pineapple juice

Dash Worcestershire sauce

1 to 2 tablespoons cornstarch
    dissolved in 1/2 cup water

1. Combine all ingredients, except cornstarch, in a saucepan and bring to a boil.

2. Add 1 tablespoon cornstarch and boil until sauce thickens. Add more cornstarch for a thicker sauce.

3. Serve with sauce poured over fish.

HAM SALAD WITH SPICY ORANGE AND PEANUT DRESSING

Serves 4

◆ Take advantage of leftover meat (beef, pork, chicken or lamb) to make a satisfying salad. If a large ham is too much, smaller cuts are available. Buy a piece with some bone left in (usually it's cheaper) and use the bone for flavoring a soup such as split pea or lentil.

3 tablespoons peanut butter, crunchy works well for texture

Juice of 1 orange, (4 to 5 tablespoons) and 1/4 rind, minced

1 large clove garlic, minced

1 small piece fresh ginger, minced

1/4 teaspoon chile flakes, or to taste

Pinch ground cloves

2 to 3 cups cooked ham or other meat, diced

1 large head lettuce, shredded

1 cucumber, peeled and thinly sliced

1 small red onion, thinly sliced

2 tablespoons parsley or cilantro, chopped, for garnish, optional

1. In a large saucepan heat peanut butter, orange juice and rind, garlic, ginger, chile flakes and cloves. Mixture should be runny. Toss in meat, stir to coat and heat through.

2. Lay lettuce and cucumber on a large platter. Add meat mixture and scatter red onion and cilantro on top.

LEG OF LAMB WITH CITRUS AND RED WINE MARINADE

Serves 12

◆ Here's a delicious alternative to the tried-and-true teriyaki and barbecue marinades. Marinating the meat or poultry overnight infuses it with flavors enhanced by cooking over charcoal. This marinade works well for leg of lamb or lowfat (and low budget) turkey breast, or even chicken.

4 to 5 pounds leg of lamb or turkey breast, butterflied, see note

6 large cloves garlic, peeled

1 orange, skin on, quartered and seeded

1 medium onion, quartered

1 tablespoon ground cumin

2 small bay leaves

1 dried red chile, optional

Small handful fresh parsley, cilantro or mint leaves

Black pepper, to taste

2 to 3 cups red wine

1/2 cup olive oil

1. Put the meat in a large plastic bag or in a container large enough to hold it and the marinade. Do not use cast iron or aluminum.

2. Add all ingredients, except wine and oil, to food processor or blender and process until well chopped. Add the wine and oil and pulse until well blended.

3. Pour marinade into bag or container. Be sure meat is evenly covered. Secure tightly and refrigerate overnight.

4. Before grilling, let meat come to room temperature for about an hour, then cooking will be very quick.

NOTE: Have the butcher butterfly the meat to remove the bone. Then the marinade soaks in easily and the cooking time is considerably shorter.

LAMB FAJITAS

Makes 8

◆ Fajitas make a fast and delicious meal. For economy, buy a leg or shoulder and cut it up for two or three meals. If the cost of peppers is high, use more onions and thinly sliced carrots for color and texture. Serve with salsa, sour cream or guacamole.

1 pound lamb or other meat,

    cut in 1-inch steaks for grill or

    strips for stir-fry

2 tablespoons olive oil

2 tablespoons fresh lime juice

3 tablespoons orange juice or tequila

1 teaspoon oregano

1 teaspoon ground cumin

1 teaspoon chile powder

Salt and pepper, to taste

1/4 teaspoon cayenne

2 tablespoons fresh cilantro

1 large onion, halved for grill or

    thinly sliced for stir-fry

1 green pepper, halved for grill or

    thinly sliced for stir-fry

1 carrot, whole for grill or thinly

    sliced for stir-fry

1 or 2 tablespoons oil for stir-fry

8 medium flour tortillas, warmed

1. Put meat in large container. Combine oil, juices, spices and cilantro in a bowl and add to meat. Marinate 4 to 6 hours, covered, in refrigerator.

2. To cook on the grill: Prepare coals and grill meat and vegetables. Meat will cook about 5 to 6 minutes on each side. Turn vegetables frequently to avoid burning.

3. Slice meat and vegetables into thin strips and serve in tortillas rolled with salsa or other condiments.

4. To stir-fry: Toss vegetables with lamb and marinade. Heat oil in large skillet. On medium high heat, stir-fry vegetables and meat about 3 to 5 minutes. Cook in two batches if necessary. Serve as in 3, above.

LAMB WITH PITA BREAD

Serves 4

◆ Here's a scrumptious alternative to hot dogs and hamburgers. Use lamb cut from the leg and grilled. Or, use already cooked meat. The horseradish and cream cheese add zip. When stuffed with crunchy cucumbers, lettuce and tomatoes, these overstuffed pita sandwiches are perfect picnic fare.

4 ounces light cream cheese

1 heaping tablespoon prepared

   horseradish, or to taste

1 tablespoon chopped fresh parsley

1 green onion, chopped or

   1 tablespoon onion, finely chopped

1 heaping tablespoon pickle relish,

   optional (but good)

4 pita breads

8 slices cooked leg of lamb, or about

   1-1/2 cups bite-size pieces of

   poultry or other meat

4 large lettuce leaves

1 medium-to-large tomato, sliced

1/2 large cucumber, peeled and sliced

Salt and pepper, to taste

1. Combine cream cheese, horseradish, parsley, onion and relish. Refrigerate for about 20 minutes.

2. To serve: Spread cheese mixture equally on each pita and add remaining ingredients.

ONION BREAD SQUARES

Makes 25 1-inch squares

◆ Make this delicious bread as a last-minute addition to any meal. To cut fat calories, use nonfat milk, lowfat sour cream, and leave out the egg yolk. Leftover bread can be frozen, reheated in the oven and served with eggs at breakfast.

4 tablespoons olive oil

2 medium onions, thinly sliced

1 teaspoon sugar

4 drops Worcestershire sauce,
**   or to taste**

Dash Tabasco sauce, or to taste

Salt and pepper, to taste

2 cups flour

1 tablespoon baking powder

1/4 teaspoon salt

3/4 teaspoon dried oregano or
**   rosemary, crushed**

2/3 cup nonfat milk

2/3 cup lowfat sour cream

1 egg (or just white)

1 tablespoon parsley or cilantro,
**   finely chopped**

1. In a skillet, heat 1 tablespoon olive oil and saute onions on medium heat until they begin to soften.

2. Add sugar, Worcestershire, Tabasco, salt and pepper. Continue cooking, stirring frequently, until completely soft. Remove from heat.

3. In a bowl, sift together flour, baking powder and salt. Add herbs and remaining 3 tablespoons olive oil. Stir with a fork until tiny beads appear. Add milk and stir until flour is absorbed. Dough will be slightly sticky.

4. With lightly floured hands, knead 10 times to incorporate all the flour.

5. Press dough into a 9 by 9 inch well-greased pan. Top with onions.

6. With a fork, mix sour cream with egg white until smooth.

7. Sprinkle top with chopped parsley and spread sour cream mixture thinly over it. Bake in preheated 400 degree oven for 20 minutes or until top begins to brown. Serve hot, cut into squares.

ONION SAUTE

Serves 4 to 6

◆ This economical, versatile and satisfying dish is wonderful with grilled meats and poultry, on garlic toasts with drinks, or as a topping for homemade pizza.

2 tablespoons olive or vegetable oil

2 medium red onions, thinly sliced

3 medium yellow onions, thinly sliced

2 medium sweet white onions or

1 each red and yellow onion,

thinly sliced

2 cloves garlic, pressed

1 heaping teaspoon dry mustard,

or to taste

1 tablespoon Worcestershire sauce,

or to taste

Salt and pepper, to taste

1 teaspoon white vinegar, or to taste

3 medium green onions, including

tops, finely chopped

2 tablespoons fresh parsley,

finely chopped

1. Heat oil in large skillet. Add onions, garlic, mustard, Worcestershire, salt and pepper. Stir often and cook until onions are soft and golden.

2. Add vinegar and cook for another minute. Taste, and adjust seasonings.

3. Serve sprinkled with green onions and parsley.

ROAST ONIONS WITH ORANGE DRESSING

Serves 4

◆ The perfect accompaniment to roast meat and poultry, these onions can be made in the microwave but they won't have the carmelized flavor that baking ensures.

4 medium red, yellow or brown onions, unpeeled

4 to 5 tablespoons olive oil

Juice and zest of 1 orange

1 small clove garlic, pressed

Dash cayenne, optional

2 tablespoons parsley, chopped

Salt and pepper, to taste

1. Rub the onions with 1 to 2 tablespoons of olive oil and place in a baking dish that holds them snugly. Roast in preheated 375 degree oven for about 1 hour or until onions are soft.

2. Reserve 1 tablespoon of chopped parsley for garnish. Combine remaining ingredients in a small saucepan and cook for 1 minute to blend the flavors.

3. Cut onions in half horizontally and lay on a platter. Pour sauce over them and sprinkle with remaining parsley. Best served warm or room temperature.

ORANGE SNAP DESSERT

Serves 4

◆ This dessert takes just minutes to prepare. It also works well with thinly sliced apples, pears, apricots or just about any fruit you'd like. And, if gingersnaps aren't a favorite, use chocolate or vanilla wafers.

4 oranges, peeled and sliced

   horizontally into circles

2 tablespoons flavored liqueur

   such as Cointreau (orange),

   Amaretto (almond),

   or apple juice

1 tablespoon sugar, optional

8 gingersnaps, crushed, leave some

   small pieces

1. In a 9-inch pie pan, overlap the oranges in a circle. Sprinkle with sugar and liqueur. Top with crushed cookies.

2. Cover with plastic wrap and microwave for 1 to 2 minutes on high or just long enough to heat the fruit and slightly melt the cookies. Serve warm.

SEE ALSO Plum Compote.

ORANGE MUFFIN TOPS

Makes about 14 muffins

◆ These easy-to-make crispy muffin tops have no bottoms; the dough is cooked on a lightly greased cookie sheet rather than muffin pans. They can be made in the morning and go well with fresh fruit and eggs cooked any style. If the eaters are divided—tops versus bottoms—cook the dough in greased muffin tins.

2 cups all-purpose flour

2/3 cup sugar

1/2 teaspoon baking soda

1-1/2 teaspoon baking powder

1 heaping teaspoon pumpkin pie
 spice or a mixture of ground
 cinnamon, cloves, and nutmeg

1/2 cup raisins

1 egg, lightly beaten

4 tablespoons butter, melted
 and cooled

4 tablespoons nonfat milk

6 tablespoons orange juice

1 tablespoon orange or
 lemon rind, grated

1 teaspoon vanilla

1. In a bowl, mix with a spoon flour, sugar, baking soda, baking powder, spices, and raisins.

2. In another bowl, mix remaining ingredients. Pour liquid mixture into flour mixture and lightly stir with spoon. Don't overmix. (It won't be entirely smooth—don't worry.)

3. Drop by tablespoonfuls onto a lightly greased cookie sheet. Bake in preheated 350 degree oven for 20 to 25 minutes or until browned and just hard.

4. Serve warm or cool. Wrap and store at room temperature. Reheat, covered with foil, on baking sheets, in preheated 350 degree oven for 10 to 15 minutes.

ORANGE-OATMEAL CHEWS

Makes about 36

◆ Easy to make ahead, these bars are great for a snack or for dessert.

1 small orange with rind, ends

   removed, finely chopped

1/4 pound butter, melted

1/2 cup brown sugar

2 tablespoons corn syrup,

   optional, see note

Dash salt

1/2 teaspoon vanilla or

   almond extract

2 cups quick-cooking oats

6 ounces semi-sweet chocolate,

   melted

1/2 cup walnuts, chopped

1. In a bowl, with a spoon mix orange, butter, brown sugar, corn syrup (if used), salt and extract. Add oats and mix well.

2. Press mixture into a well-greased 9 by 9 inch square pan.

3. Bake in preheated 400 degree oven for 10 minutes, no longer. Cool slightly.

4. Spread melted chocolate over top and press walnuts into chocolate. Cover and chill.

5. To serve, cut into bite-size pieces.

NOTE: Corn syrup makes the bars chewy.

PASTA CASSEROLE

Serves 4 to 6

◆ Perfect for breakfast or a light lunch, this dish is a meal in itself. It's versatile enough to be served with roasted meat or chicken, or even served as dessert. I've used lowfat cheese and light sour cream to lower the calories and fat.

6 ounces wide dried egg noodles

1/2 cup light sour cream

1/2 cup lowfat ricotta cheese

1 egg

1 apple, cored and diced

1/3 cup raisins

1/2 cup chopped walnuts, optional

2 tablespoons sugar

Dash salt

3/4 teaspoon ground cinnamon

1/2 teaspoon vanilla

1. Cook noodles according to package directions.

2. Put all remaining ingredients into a bowl and mix thoroughly. Add noodles, mix and taste to correct seasoning.

3. Pour into an 8 by 8 inch buttered pan. Bake in preheated 350 degree oven for about 40 minutes or until top is browned.

Everything you see, I owe to spaghetti.

—SOPHIA LOREN

ASIAN FLAVORED PASTA SALAD

Serves 4 to 6

◆ For last-minute or make-ahead dishes, I always keep pasta in my cupboard. Use shrimp, meat, poultry or just vegetables in it. For color and crunch, serve the salad on lettuce or cabbage leaves.

1 pound cooked pasta such as shells
    or butterflies

2 to 3 tablespoons Oriental sesame oil

1 tablespoon vegetable oil

1 slice fresh ginger, finely chopped

2 large cloves garlic, finely chopped

1 green pepper, thinly sliced

1/3 pound shrimp, peeled, deveined
    and sliced in half horizontally,
    see note

1 bunch green onions, chopped

Zest and juice of 1 large orange

1 tablespoon salted Chinese black
    beans, crushed, optional (but
    good), see note

1/2 teaspoon dried chile flakes

2 tablespoons white vinegar

1/4 cup cilantro, chopped

1. In a large bowl, mix pasta with 1 tablespoon sesame oil. Set aside.

2. In a large skillet, heat vegetable oil and saute ginger and garlic for about 30 seconds. Add green pepper and shrimp, then saute on high for 1 or 2 minutes or until shrimp turn pink. Remove to pasta bowl.

3. In a saucepan put 1 tablespoon sesame oil, green onions, orange zest and juice, black beans and chile flakes. Gently heat until zest and chile flakes give off fragrance, about 30 seconds to 1 minute. Do not use high heat as sesame oil will burn. Add to salad.

4. Toss salad, add vinegar and cilantro and taste to correct seasoning. Chill. Serve on red cabbage leaves or red leaf lettuce, if desired.

NOTE: Leftover cooked meats will work, shredded or cubed, as will raw meat, cut into small pieces and cooked as above. Use 2 teaspoons soy sauce if salted black beans are unavailable. Look for beans in Oriental section of supermarket.

SWEET PEA GUACAMOLE

Serves 6

◆ The high price of avocados makes guacamole a dish that can dent a food budget. This delicious, easy, and unusual dip—its main ingredient is frozen sweet peas—is adapted from *Secret Ingredients* by Michael Roberts, chef at Trumps restaurant in Los Angeles. A pound of frozen peas is about $1, peas won't discolor like avocados, and they don't have the fat content of avocados. To dip, use homemade baked tortilla chips and a tray of raw vegetables such as tomatoes, green pepper and jicama. Or, use the guacamole as a side dish with grilled chicken, or as a topping for tostadas.

1/4 bunch cilantro, trimmed

1 clove garlic

1 jalapeño pepper or dried chile

   flakes, to taste

1 pound defrosted peas

1 to 2 tablespoons olive oil

2 tablespoons fresh lemon or

   lime juice

1/2 teaspoon ground cumin,

   or to taste

Pinch salt

1/4 red onion, finely diced, or

   3 green onions, finely chopped

2 small tomatoes, seeded and

   finely diced, optional

Any of your favorite guacamole

   additions such as salsa or

   sour cream, optional

1. In a food processor or blender, process the cilantro, garlic and jalapeño until roughly pureed.

2. Add peas, olive oil, lemon juice, cumin, and salt and blend until smooth. Adjust seasoning. There may be some lumps but it adds to the textural interest of the gua-camole.

3. Put into serving bowl and sprin-kle with onion, tomato, or mix onion and tomato into the pea mixture.

SEE ALSO White Bean Chile for homemade tortilla chip recipe.

NO-BAKE PEACH PIE

Serves 6 to 8

◆ This pie is a perfect summer dessert because it needs no baking and uses the season's delicious fruits such as peaches, berries, and plums.

The cost of a prepared graham cracker crust averages $1.35, while a box of graham crackers (for three pies) costs anywhere from $1.45 to over $2. And, depending on your diet, lowfat sour cream, regular sour cream, or a mix of lowfat sour cream and unflavored yogurt all work well.

8 ounces sour cream, regular
or lowfat
2 tablespoons sugar, or to taste
1/4 teaspoon each vanilla and lemon
extract, or 1/2 teaspoon of either
Zest of 1/2 orange or lemon, to taste,
optional
1 graham cracker pie crust,
see note
1 tablespoon lemon juice,
optional, see note

4 cups fresh fruit such as peaches,
berries, plums or a mixture, sliced
1 to 2 tablespoons powdered or
brown sugar, to taste, optional

1. In a bowl, mix sour cream, sugar, extracts and zest until creamy.

2. Spread mixture carefully into pie shell. Mix lemon juice with fruit and lay fruit on sour cream.

3. Refrigerate at least 1 hour, preferably longer. Serve topped with sugar, if desired.

NOTE: Crust can be homemade from 1 inner package of graham crackers, crushed, mixed with 4 tablespoons melted butter, and pressed into an 8-inch pie pan. Lemon juice keeps peaches from turning brown.

POACHED PEARS

Serves 4

◆ Poaching is a simple and versatile way to make a fruit dessert. Cooking in the microwave shaves time. The pears are great with a dollop of whipped cream or ice cream for a richer dessert, or served over angel food cake.

1 cup water and 1 cup red wine

   (if you don't have wine, use apple

   juice or even orange juice)

1 stick cinnamon or a large pinch

   ground

5 or 6 whole cloves or a

   pinch ground

2 to 3 tablespoons sugar,

   or to taste

4 pears, peeled and cut in half

   with seeds removed

1. In a saucepan, bring all ingredients but pears to a boil.

2. Add pears, turn to simmer and gently poach about 5 to 10 minutes.

3. Serve warm or room temperature.

VARIATIONS: Add juice and zest of an orange instead of wine. Add 1 teaspoon fresh ginger, grated, in place of cinnamon and cloves.

Use peaches, apples or nectarines instead of pears.

PEAR-GINGER MUFFINS

Makes 12 to 14

◆ In the fall, fresh pears and apples are easily found, at prices well within a food budget. This easy-to-make pear (or apple) muffin is perfumed with ginger and cinnamon and complements a turkey dinner or a simple breakfast.

2 cups all-purpose flour

1 teaspoon baking soda

1/4 teaspoon salt

1/3 cup brown sugar

2 teaspoons ground ginger

1 teaspoon ground cinnamon

1/8 teaspoon each ground cloves
    and nutmeg

1 egg, beaten

1 cup low or nonfat plain yogurt

1/3 cup oil

2 large pears, peeled, cored and
    diced, about 1-3/4 cups, or use
    apples or a combination of both

1/3 cup raisins

1/3 cup walnuts, chopped

1. Sift flour, baking soda and salt into large bowl. Add remaining dry ingredients and mix well.

2. Add egg, yogurt and oil. Stir. Add pears, raisins and walnuts and mix with a fork.

3. Fill buttered and floured muffin cups 2/3 full. Bake in preheated 375 degree oven for 20 to 25 minutes or until toothpick comes out clean.

PLUM COMPOTE

Serves 4 to 6

◆ Summer fruits such as plums and grapes are great for eating raw or cooked. For a change of pace, try this compote to eat alone, for breakfast over cereal, or for dessert over ice cream or angel food cake. Vary the type and quantity of the fruits.

2 pounds fresh plums, halved
  and pitted

1 bunch grapes, stemmed

1 green apple, cored and chopped

2 bananas, cut in 1-inch slices

1 orange, peeled, seeded and
  sectioned

Juice of 2 oranges, plus zest of 1

3/4 cup red wine or fruit juice

Dash sugar, optional

Pinch cinnamon, optional

1. Put all ingredients into a large stainless steel pot and cook covered until fruit softens. If there is too much liquid, uncover the pot, turn up heat for a few minutes to reduce the liquid.

2. Serve hot, at room temperature or cold.

ORIENTAL PORK AND VEGETABLE SALAD

Serves 4 to 6

◆ The vegetables in this summer salad can be raw, but stir-frying gives them a refreshing change in taste and texture.

1 2-ounce package cellophane
   noodles (also called vermicelli,
   mung bean or glass noodles),
   see note
1/2 head lettuce, coarsely shredded
2 to 3 tablespoons vegetable oil
2 large cucumbers, peeled, cut in
   half horizontally, seeded, and cut
   into 1-inch pieces
2 stalks celery, chopped
1/2 head red cabbage, coarsely
   shredded
4 green onions, chopped
1/2 green pepper, julienned, optional
2 to 3 cups leftover roasted or grilled
   pork, chicken, beef or 1/2 pound
   cooked shrimp

1 cup bean sprouts
1/2 cup toasted sesame seeds or
   crushed peanuts, optional
3 tablespoons cilantro, chopped,
   optional

1. Soak noodles in hot water for 5 to 10 minutes or until soft.

2. Spread noodles on a large serving platter and sprinkle lettuce over them. Set aside.

3. Heat 1 tablespoon oil in a skillet or wok and stir-fry vegetables (except bean sprouts) in batches, adding additional oil as necessary. Stir-fry on high for 1 to 2 minutes or until vegetables soften.

4. Remove to large bowl, add meat and dressing. Mix well and arrange over noodles. Sprinkle with bean sprouts, nuts and cilantro. Chill and serve.

NOTE: Noodles are available in Oriental section of supermarket.

ORIENTAL PORK AND VEGETABLE SALAD *(continued)*

ORIENTAL STYLE DRESSING

1 clove garlic, pressed

1/2-inch fresh ginger, minced

3 tablespoons sesame oil

Pinch sugar

6 tablespoons white vinegar

Black pepper, to taste

Dash soy sauce, to taste, optional

1/2 teaspoon dried chile flakes, to
   taste, optional

Blend all ingredients and toss
with salad.

> *Better a man should wait*
>
> *for a dish than a dish*
>
> *should wait for a man.*
>
> —CHINESE PROVERB

PORK AND MUSHROOM STIR-FRY, ITALIAN STYLE

Serves 4

◆ The trick with stir-fry is small pieces of food, constantly stirred and cooked quickly on a high heat. This recipe takes the stir-fry method and teams it with pork (chicken also works well), mushrooms and Italian herbs instead of the usual Asian flavors of garlic, ginger and soy.

1 to 2 tablespoons olive or

vegetable oil

1 medium onion, quartered and

separated

1 large clove garlic, pressed

1 pound pork, cut in small pieces

8 medium mushrooms, thinly sliced,

see note

2 teaspoons oregano, basil or favorite

herb, fresh or dried, or to taste

Salt and pepper, to taste

1 carrot, shredded

4 tablespoons chopped parsley

3 to 4 tablespoons white wine or

chicken broth

1. Heat oil in large skillet or wok on medium high heat. Add onion and stir constantly as the onion begins to soften.

2. Add garlic to meat, mix and then toss into wok, continue stirring and cook until pork begins to lose its color. Add mushrooms, herbs, salt and pepper and continue stirring.

3. Add carrot, two tablespoons parsley, and wine or broth. Continue stirring. Taste and adjust seasoning.

4. Serve on a bed of oven-roasted rosemary potatoes, or rice. Sprinkle remaining parsley on top.

VARIATIONS: Additional vegetables such as a slivered half red pepper, broccoli, snow peas, or a few cherry tomatoes could also be added.

SEE ALSO Baked Potatoes with Variations for Oven Roasted Potatoes.

POTATOES WITH CAESAR STYLE DRESSING

Serves 4 to 6

◆ A simple Caesar style dressing coats potatoes instead of greens for an easy and unusual salad. A bottled dressing works, but it may dent your budget and it won't have the tang created by fresh lemon juice, olive oil and garlic.

Juice of 2 lemons

Zest of 1 lemon, optional

4 to 5 tablespoons olive oil

1 tablespoon wine vinegar

3 green onions, finely chopped

4 tablespoons fresh parsley,

finely chopped

1 to 2 anchovies, mashed, to taste,

optional

4 to 6 tablespoons Parmesan cheese

Salt and pepper, to taste

Dash Worcestershire sauce

2 pounds potatoes, peeled, cooked

and cut into small chunks

1/2 cup croutons, optional

1. In a bowl, combine all ingredients except potatoes. Adjust seasoning.

2. Add potatoes.

3. Top with croutons and serve. Can be served chilled or at room temperature.

ORIENTAL POTATO SALAD

Serves 6 to 8

◆ For picnics and tailgate parties I often think of potato salad. Here, the usual mayonnaise-based dressing that can spoil without refrigeration is replaced with Asian flavors of garlic, ginger, sesame oil and vinegar that travel well. Expand the salad with leftover grilled chicken, turkey or meat and serve on a bed of lettuce or shredded red cabbage for color and texture.

5 pounds potatoes, boiled, cooled, peeled (if desired), chunked

1 carrot, shredded, see note

1 bunch green onions, chopped, use half for dressing

1. Mix all ingredients in a large bowl.

THE DRESSING

2 to 3 cloves garlic, pressed

1 piece fresh ginger, chopped, approximately 1 tablespoon

1/2 cup white vinegar

2 tablespoons Oriental sesame oil

Juice and zest of 1 orange

Dash sugar

Dash soy, to taste, optional

2 teaspoons salted black beans, crushed, see note

1 teaspoons dried pepper flakes or 1/2 teaspoon cayenne, optional

Pinch Chinese 5-spice powder, optional

3 to 4 tablespoons cilantro, chopped

1. In a saucepan put 1/2 chopped green onions and dressing ingredients except cilantro. Bring to a boil and cook for one minute to release flavors. Cool slightly and pour over potatoes. Toss with cilantro and remaining green onion.

NOTE: I like shredded carrot for color and crunch. Radishes or water chestnuts would also work. Salted black beans are found in the Oriental foods section of the supermarket.

POTATO SALAD WITH ORANGE-MINT DRESSING

Serves 4

◆ This refreshing variation of potato salad uses leftover chicken or meat. Try to make the salad ahead of time so the flavors can meld.

3 pounds potatoes, boiled, peeled
  (if desired), chunked
1 carrot, shredded
1 red onion, finely sliced
Salt and pepper, to taste
1 pound (approx) leftover roasted or
  grilled chicken, beef or pork,
  cubed, optional

1. Mix all ingredients in a large bowl.

ORANGE-MINT DRESSING

Juice and zest of 2 oranges, reserve
  zest of 1 orange as garnish
2 tablespoons fresh mint, finely
  chopped or 1 teaspoon dried
6 tablespoons olive oil
2 tablespoons white vinegar
1 clove garlic, pressed
1/8 teaspoon ground cinnamon,
  or to taste
Fresh ground pepper, to taste

1. Mix all dressing ingredients, except reserved zest, together in a jar and shake.

2. Let stand for 15 minutes so flavors blend.

3. To serve, mix dressing with salad and sprinkle with reserved zest.

MASHED POTATOES WITH LEMON AND GARLIC

Serves 4 to 6

◆ Potatoes rank high on my list of simple comfort foods. I always have them on hand to bake or boil for salads or soups. They add versatility to any menu and are as gentle on a waistline (if not overloaded with butter and sour cream) as they are on a budget's bottom line.

Mashed potatoes are a cinch to make. This addictive version can be used as a side dish or thinned for a sauce. Use boiling potatoes or the more starchy russets, but don't use a food processor to beat them—they will become gluey.

6 to 8 cloves garlic, pressed

Dash salt, or to taste

2 pounds potatoes or 1 medium potato per person, peeled, cut and boiled, save cooking water

2 to 3 tablespoons olive oil

2 to 3 tablespoons lemon juice

White or black pepper, to taste

2 tablespoons parsley, minced, optional

1. Mix garlic and salt together to make a paste.

2. Mash potatoes with a masher or electric beater, using the potato water to thin as desired. Add olive oil, lemon juice, and adjust seasoning. Serve garnished with parsley, as desired.

VARIATION: Use milk and butter instead of olive oil and lemon juice.

What I say is that,

if a man really

likes potatoes,

he must be a pretty

decent sort of fellow.

—A.A. MILNE

POTATO AND SPINACH SOUP

Serves 4 to 6

◆ With the addition of sausage this toothsome soup becomes a meal-in-one. If sausage isn't a favorite, leave it out and serve the soup as part of a meal with poultry or meat.

1 tablespoon olive oil

1 onion, finely chopped

1 clove garlic, pressed

4 medium-to-large russet potatoes, peeled, chunked

8 cups water or broth

Salt and pepper, to taste

Pinch Italian herbs, to taste

1 bunch spinach, washed, stemmed, finely shredded

1/2 pound Italian sausage, cooked and sliced thinly, optional

1. In a large saucepan, heat oil and saute onion and garlic for a minute.

2. Add potatoes, water, salt, pepper and herbs. Cover and boil until potatoes are soft but not mushy, about 15 minutes.

3. Drain, but reserve the liquid. Mash potatoes in the pan with a fork or masher and add the reserved liquid.

4. Bring to a boil, add spinach and cook about 2 minutes or until the spinach is wilted but still bright green.

5. Add sausage and taste to adjust seasoning.

SAVORY POTATO PANCAKES

Serves 4

◆ With a salad or vegetable, these pancakes make the meal, especially topped with homemade applesauce or cinnamon and sugar. For a more substantial meal, add roasted chicken or meat.

6 medium potatoes, finely shredded

    and drained, see note

1 large onion, finely shredded

    and drained

Pinch baking soda

2 tablespoons flour

2 eggs

2 tablespoons parsley, finely chopped

1/2 teaspoon grated nutmeg,

    cinnamon or clove, to taste,

    optional

Salt and pepper, to taste

4 to 6 tablespoons olive oil, butter

    or mixture of both

1. Mix all ingredients, except oil or butter, in a large bowl. Taste to adjust seasoning.

2. Heat 1 tablespoon oil in a large skillet, or use non-stick pan with less oil. When hot, drop potato mixture by tablespoonfuls onto skillet. Fry until brown on both sides.

NOTE: Potatoes can be peeled, but I like the additional flavor of the peel. Also, for a different texture, potatoes can be finely chopped in a food processor. Grating adds another dimension.

BAKED POTATOES WITH VARIATIONS

Serves 8

◆ Baked potatoes are delicious plain, slathered with butter and sour cream or restuffed with vegetables, eggs or cheese. Once baked they can be cut in chunks and roasted in the oven.

BAKED

1 potato per person, preferably russet, scrubbed, ends removed

1. Bake in a preheated 400 degree oven for 40 to 60 minutes depending on size. Potatoes should be soft when pushed with fingers. Prick them once with a fork halfway through cooking, if desired, to release steam and make the flesh flaky.

2. Or cook in microwave oven according to manufacturer's instructions, usually about 7 minutes on high. Be sure to prick potatoes with a fork before cooking so they won't burst as they cook.

RESTUFFED

8 medium or 4 large potatoes, baked

1/4 cup milk

1 6-ounce jar marinated artichoke hearts, drained, finely chopped

1 tablespoon parsley, finely chopped

1 clove garlic, pressed

Salt and pepper, to taste

1. Cut baked potato in half and scoop out pulp. Put into a bowl and moisten with a little milk.

2. Add remaining ingredients. Mash. Restuff potatoes and bake in preheated 400 degree oven until tops are golden.

OVEN ROASTED

Chunk baked potatoes and toss in ovenproof skillet with 4 tablespoons olive oil and a large pinch crushed dried rosemary. Salt and pepper to taste, and bake in preheated 375 degree oven, stirring occasionally until potatoes begin to crisp about 20 to 30 minutes.

PUMPKIN-ORANGE MUFFINS

Makes 18 to 20

◆ Pumpkin is great to use because it comes, without additives, in one-pound cans at a cost of just under $1. These dense, moist muffins are easy to make, have no cholesterol, and can be tailored to taste. If pumpkin isn't available, banana also works well.

1 orange, ends removed, seeded, and
   pureed in food processor

2 cups pumpkin puree or 3 ripe
   bananas, mashed

1/4 cup sugar

4 tablespoons vegetable oil

3 tablespoons milk

2 egg whites, slightly beaten

2 cups flour

1-1/2 teaspoons baking powder

1 teaspoon baking soda

1 teaspoon ground cinnamon

1/4 teaspoon ground nutmeg
   or cloves, optional

Dash salt

1/3 cup raisins, chopped walnuts,
   chocolate chips, or a mixture

1. Mix all ingredients in a bowl.

2. Fill well-greased muffin tins about 1/2 full. Bake in preheated · 375 degree oven for 20 to 30 minutes or until golden on top. The pumpkin takes longer to bake than the banana.

PUMPKIN CUSTARD

Serves 8

◆ Perfect for Thanksgiving, this custard is an easy alternative to the usual pumpkin pie.

3 eggs, lightly beaten

2 cups milk

1 cup pumpkin puree

3 tablespoons honey

1 teaspoon pumpkin pie spice or

   a mixture of cinnamon, cloves

   and nutmeg

1. Combine all ingredients and beat with a fork until smooth.

2. Pour into 8 buttered custard cups. Place cups in a pan and fill with enough hot water to reach 1 inch up the sides of the cups.

3. Bake in preheated 325 degree oven for 20 to 25 minutes or until custard is set and a knife inserted in the center comes out clean. Remove from water, cool slightly and refrigerate.

4. Serve with Chocolate Dipped Figs, if desired.

CONFETTI RICE SALAD

Serves 4

◆ Rice is a low cost, healthful base for this salad using garden fresh tomatoes, cucumbers and herbs—simple yet satisfying summer flavors. Vary the vegetables and herbs and serve as a light lunch or as a side dish to grilled meat.

3 cups cooked rice, see

   Easy Rice recipe

1 small carrot, shredded

2 medium tomatoes, seeded, diced

1 cucumber, peeled, seeded, finely

   chopped

1 small red onion, thinly sliced

1/2 cup raisins

1/2 cup walnuts or almonds,

   chopped

1. Mix all ingredients in a large bowl.

LEMON DRESSING

3 tablespoons olive oil

Juice and zest of two lemons

Dash of wine vinegar, to taste,

   optional

1 clove garlic, pressed

1/4 cup, (approx.) mixed fresh herbs

   such as parsley, thyme, oregano,

   basil or cilantro

Salt and pepper, to taste

1. Mix all dressing ingredients. Taste to correct seasoning.

2. Mix with rice mixture. Chill and serve.

NOTE: Can be used to stuff artichokes, tomatoes or green peppers.

EASY RICE

Serves 4

◆ Rice is one of the most versatile and inexpensive foods in the cupboard. Raw rice that is, not the prepackaged kind with seasonings already added. It takes the same 20 minutes to cook raw rice as it does to make the boxed version. And raw rice can be flavored to taste.

Make this dish plain as the base for a salad or flavored with any dried herb seasonings such as Italian, Mexican or even curry to go with grilled meats or vegetables.

1 tablespoon olive or vegetable oil

1/2 onion, finely diced

1/2 teaspoon herb seasoning, as

   desired, to taste

1/2 teaspoon salt, to taste

1 cup raw rice

2 cups water or chicken stock

1. Heat oil in a large saucepan, and add onion. Cook until it begins to soften, about 1 minute.

2. Add herbs, salt and rice. Stir until the grains are coated.

3. Add water. Bring to a boil, cover, turn heat down to simmer and cook 20 minutes or until all liquid is absorbed.

4. Remove from heat and let rest a few minutes with the lid on. Makes 3 cups.

SHRIMP-CHICKEN STIR-FRY

Serves 4

◆ One way to use shrimp without going over budget is to include it in a stir-fry with vegetables and chicken. Look for specials on shrimp—they're cheaper shell-on and raw rather than already peeled and cooked. Cut them in half horizontally or in pieces to stretch a small quantity. Serve the stir-fry with rice and a fruit dessert.

2 to 3 tablespoons vegetable oil

1/3 pound shrimp, peeled, deveined and cut horizontally or in pieces.

2 cups chicken, cut in bite-size pieces (use breast or thigh meat)

1/4 cup water or stock

1 pound broccoli, cut in bite-size pieces

1 onion, thinly sliced

2 cloves garlic, minced

2 teaspoons curry powder, to taste, optional

Dash soy or salt, to taste

Pinch sugar, to taste

1. In a wok or large skillet, heat 1 tablespoon oil and stir-fry shrimp until pink. Remove to bowl.

2. Add chicken to wok and stir-fry until it turns white, approximately 2 minutes. Remove to bowl with shrimp.

3. Add water and broccoli to wok, cover and cook about 2 minutes. Broccoli should remain crisp. Remove and add to shrimp and chicken.

4. Add 1 tablespoon oil, onion, garlic and seasonings to wok, stir-fry until onion softens, then add shrimp, chicken, and broccoli. Stir-fry about 1 minute to heat and mix. Adjust seasoning.

SPAGHETTI SQUASH WITH GARLIC AND OLIVE OIL

Serves 4

◆ Colorful winter squash (such as acorn, butternut, hubbard or spaghetti) are good buys in the winter. While most of them can be steamed or baked and then peeled so the flesh can be mashed, the spaghetti squash yields flesh that looks like strands of pasta. It works well with tomato sauce, vegetables and other simple pasta sauces.

1 4-pound spaghetti squash

4 tablespoons olive oil

1/2 onion, thinly sliced

1/2 carrot, shredded

1 cup leftover meat or poultry,

   shredded or cubed, optional

4 mushrooms, thinly sliced

2 cloves garlic, pressed

Juice of 1 lemon, or to taste

Salt and pepper

3 tablespoons parsley,

   finely chopped

Parmesan cheese, optional

1. Fill a large pot with water and put in the whole squash. Cover and cook on medium high for approximately 20 minutes or until a fork goes through the skin. Or, cook in microwave oven according to the manufacturer's instructions.

2. Remove from water, cut in half horizontally, scoop out seeds and with a fork lift the strands of squash into a bowl.

3. Quickly saute onion, carrot, meat and mushrooms in 1 tablespoon of oil. Meanwhile, in a separate saucepan heat remaining oil with garlic; but do not let garlic fry or turn color.

4. Add onion mixture to squash in bowl and toss with warmed garlic and olive oil. Taste and adjust seasoning with lemon juice, salt, pepper and parsley. Serve with grated Parmesan cheese if desired.

SQUASH PANCAKES

Makes 22 to 24 small pancakes

◆ For winter eating, hard-shell squash such as banana, acorn, butternut or pumpkin (canned) are a good buy. This recipe makes a delicious side dish for roasted meats and poultry. The recipe is adapted from Faye Levy's *Fresh From France*.

1 onion, finely chopped or 1 bunch

    green onion, finely chopped

4 tablespoons oil, or use non-stick

    skillet

1/2-pound winter squash, cooked

    peeled, squeezed of moisture, see

    note, or 8 ounces canned pumpkin

1 bunch fresh spinach, washed,

    stemmed, steamed, and squeezed

    of moisture, see note

1/2 cup flour

2 eggs (1 yolk and 2 whites if

    watching cholesterol)

Freshly grated nutmeg

Salt and pepper, to taste

1. Heat 1 tablespoon oil in skillet and saute onion until soft. Remove onion and put in a bowl with cooked squash and spinach.

2. In another bowl mix flour, eggs, nutmeg, salt and pepper to a thick batter. Add to the vegetables. Mix to coat.

3. Heat 1 to 2 tablespoons remaining oil, or use non-stick skillet and drop pancakes by tablespoonful into pan. Fry gently. Turn pancakes to brown on other side.

NOTE: Cook squash and spinach in microwave until soft or steam on the stove until soft. Spinach will take only a minute or two to wilt in the microwave.

ACORN SQUASH FILLED WITH PEARS

Serves 4

◆ Healthy and affordable, winter squash makes a colorful main course, soup or even pie. Pumpkin, spaghetti, turban, acorn and banana are some of the winter squash varieties available. They are easy to prepare—usually microwaved, boiled or baked—and take well to most spices, particularly nutmeg, cinnamon and cloves. This easy dish is adapted from Nika Hazelton's *What Shall I Cook Today?*

2 tablespoons butter

1 large onion, finely chopped

1 small piece fresh ginger, chopped, or about 1/2 teaspoon to 1 teaspoon ground ginger

1/2 teaspoon ground nutmeg

2 tablespoons brown sugar

2-1/2 tablespoons bourbon or water

Salt and pepper, to taste

1 large pear, peeled, cored, finely diced, or an apple

2 acorn squash, cut lengthwise, seeded, cooked until almost soft

1. Heat butter in frying pan and saute onion until soft. Stir in ginger, nutmeg, sugar and bourbon, salt, pepper, and fruit. Cook about 3 minutes, adjust seasoning.

2. Fill squash halves, cover and finish cooking in preheated 400 degree oven, about 10 minutes, or microwave on high for 1 to 2 minutes or until squash is soft.

VARIATION: Stuff with rice or couscous.

COOL TOMATO-VEGETABLE SOUP

Serves 4 to 6

◆ The abundance of garden fresh cucumbers and tomatoes make this cool summer soup a cinch. Pack it in a thermos to take on a picnic or serve it with crusty bread and grilled foods. Vary the spicing according to taste; cumin or dill work well.

4 large tomatoes, seeded, finely
   chopped
1 large cucumber, peeled, seeded,
   finely chopped
1 medium red onion, finely chopped
1 green pepper, seeded, 3/4 of it
   chopped, remaining 1/4 sliced in
   thin strips
1 clove garlic, pressed
4 tablespoons olive oil
4 tablespoons wine vinegar
1 6-ounce can tomato juice
1 cup ice water
Dash Worcestershire sauce
1 teaspoon ground cumin or fresh
   dill, chopped

Pinch celery seed, optional
1 tablespoon chopped parsley or
   cilantro, optional
Salt and pepper, to taste

1. In a bowl combine all ingredients except sliced green pepper.

2. Taste to correct seasoning.

3. Chill at least 4 hours and serve in chilled mugs or bowls, topped with green pepper strips.

VARIATION: Make this soup in a processor or blender, but take care to use quick pulses to leave some lumps.

TORTILLA SANDWICH ROLLS

Serves 4

◆ A ham and cheese sandwich in a tortilla? Absolutely. Flour tortillas are a low-cost alternative to bread. Look for flour tortillas made with vegetable oil rather than lard. They need no heating and a large package serves 8 to 10 people for about $1.50. Make these sandwich rolls ahead of time to take on a picnic—or put in a lunchbox—and serve them with salad and dessert. Use different textures like crunchy lettuce, onions and cucumbers to balance the softness of the tortilla and its meat filling. This roll has an Asian flavor twist.

4 large flour tortillas

4 large lettuce leaves, washed, dried

Small handful fresh bean sprouts

1 small cucumber, peeled,
   thinly sliced

1/2 red onion, finely chopped

Small handful fresh cilantro, chopped

1/2 pound, (approx.) cooked chicken,
   pork or beef, preferably sliced

DRESSING

1 tablespoon sesame oil, or to taste

3 tablespoons white vinegar

1 large clove garlic, pressed

Pinch chile flakes, or to taste

Dash mustard, or to taste

1. Mix dressing ingredients.

2. Lay tortillas flat. Place a lettuce leaf on lower third of each tortilla.

3. Mix remaining ingredients with dressing.

4. Evenly distribute filling between the lettuce leaves. Don't use too much dressing if making ahead—the tortilla may get soggy.

5. Fold like an envelope (or burrito) by folding lower third over filling, then overlapping each side onto the filling and finally turning over.

6. Slice roll diagonally so it can be arranged on a plate.

SEE ALSO Egg and Artichoke Burrito, Lamb Fajitas, and Tortilla Chips.

UNDER-THE-SKIN TURKEY

Serves 6 to 8

◆ Whether whole or in parts, turkey is available year-round, and it's an economical, light, and nutritious meat. For the summer months, it's convenient to throw on the barbecue and use leftovers for salads, sandwiches or soups. Like chicken, a whole turkey is a good buy. Already cut parts, however, save cooking time and are more economical for smaller households. The trick with this recipe is to put the flavors under the skin, so that they permeate the meat as it cooks.

1 turkey breast or 4 legs or 4 thighs

1 handful fresh parsley,
   finely minced

2 cloves garlic, finely minced

2 to 4 tablespoons olive oil

1 teaspoon herbs, Italian or Mexican
   seasonings, oregano or your
   favorite

1 orange, thinly sliced

1. Gently run your hand under turkey skin to loosen it from the meat. Do not remove skin, simply loosen it.

2. Mix parsley, garlic, olive oil and herbs together. Dip the orange slices in the mixture to coat, and then gently shove them under the skin.

3. Bake or barbecue in moderate heat (about 350 degrees) 30 minutes or more, depending on size of turkey pieces. It's done when meat is firm to the touch and juices run clear, not pink, when pricked with a fork.

VARIATIONS: Use your favorite seasonings, or lemon instead of orange for a change. Also, chicken works in place of turkey.

TURKEY HASH

Serves 4 to 6

◆ Hash makes quick and convenient use of leftover meats and vegetables. Add a poached egg on top for brunch, or serve it with a salad and fruit for lunch or dinner. This recipe is adapted from James Beard—his additions were almonds and black olives—and it works well with leftover turkey and stuffing.

2 to 4 tablespoons olive or vegetable

　oil, butter or a mixture

1 small onion, finely chopped

1/2 green pepper, seeded,

　finely chopped

2 to 3 cloves garlic, pressed or

　finely chopped

3 cups diced cooked turkey

1 cup stuffing

Salt and pepper, to taste, or optional

　seasonings such as curry powder,

　Mexican or Italian blends

1/2 cup toasted almonds,

　coarsely chopped

1/2 cup pitted black olives, chopped

1/2 to 2/3 cup cream, optional

1 tablespoon parsley, for garnish,

　optional

1. In a skillet (I used a cast iron one for a crusty bottom layer of hash), heat olive oil and saute onion, pepper and garlic. Cook until soft and slightly browned.

2. Add remaining ingredients and mix well. Cook slowly so that a crust forms on the bottom. Or, pour cream over the hash so it dribbles to the bottom to form a richer crust.

3. Either way, serve from the skillet or invert onto a plate and sprinkle with chopped parsley.

VARIATIONS: Substitute other vegetables such as pearl onions, celery, shredded carrot or leftover rice and potatoes. Check the pantry for other possible additions such as marinated artichoke hearts, water chestnuts, even a small handful of capers. Finish with butter and cream for a richer hash.

TURKEY PICADILLO

Serves 4

◆ Variations abound for creative one-dish meals using ground meat, fruit and nuts. The diversity comes from herbs and spices—rosemary, sage and garlic for an Italian twist, or this slightly sweet Mexican blend with cinnamon, oregano and chiles. This do-ahead dish is perfect for tamales, tacos, burritos, or stuffed in green peppers.

1 tablespoon olive or vegetable oil

1 medium onion, finely chopped

1 large clove garlic, minced

  or pressed

1 pound ground turkey, beef or pork

1 generous cup canned or fresh

  tomatoes, chopped

1/2 teaspoon chile flakes or 1

  jalapeño chile, chopped, or to taste

1 carrot, grated

1/3 cup raisins

1 small apple, cored and chopped

1/4 teaspoon cinnamon, or to taste

1/2 teaspoon oregano, or to taste

Salt and pepper, to taste

2 tablespoons vinegar, or to taste

1/3 cup almonds, cashews, walnuts or

  pinenuts, roasted and chopped

2 tablespoons parsley or cilantro,

  chopped for garnish

1. Heat oil in large skillet, add onion, garlic and meat. Saute until meat loses color and onions soften. Drain fat if necessary.

2. Add remaining ingredients except vinegar, nuts and parsley. Cover and cook about 15 minutes. Taste and adjust seasonings.

3. Add vinegar and taste. There should be a subtle balance of flavors.

4. Just before serving, mix in nuts and top with parsley or cilantro. Serve with rice.

TURKEY LOAF

Makes 8 to 10 slices

◆ This economical variation on meatloaf uses ground turkey in place of red meat. Ground turkey is low in fat and because it has little waste, it's a good buy pound per pound. The orange slices (or apple) and the curry add zip. Use a ring mold or a loaf pan and serve it hot with a vegetable or salad or cold with a sweet and hot mustard.

1 pound ground turkey

1 stalk celery, chopped

2 cloves garlic, pressed

1/2-inch piece fresh ginger, finely

   minced, optional

1 small onion, chopped

1/4 cup parsley, chopped

1 egg

3 cups cooked rice, see Easy Rice

2 teaspoons curry powder,

   or to taste, see note

Salt and pepper, to taste

1 orange or apple, thinly sliced

1 tablespoon fresh parsley or

   cilantro, chopped

1. In a large bowl, mix all ingredients except orange and parsley.

2. Finely chop two orange slices and add to poultry mixture, mix and adjust seasoning. Halve the remaining orange slices.

3. Oil a 10-inch ring mold or a loaf pan. Line the pan with orange slices and fill the mold.

4. Bake for 40 to 45 minutes in preheated 350 degree oven. Remove from oven and let rest for 5 minutes. Place a plate over the pan and invert so orange slices are on top. Sprinkle with parsley.

NOTE: Italian herb seasoning can be substituted; if doing so, omit the ginger.

WINTER VEGETABLES WITH HORSERADISH-DILL SAUCE

Serves 4 to 6

◆ Winter root vegetables such as carrots, potatoes, turnips and rutabagas usually wind up as filler in the stew pot rather than the main attraction. Here the vegetables meet in a side dish perfect with any meat or poultry. The dish works well with any combination of vegetables.

4 to 5 medium potatoes, steamed or boiled, peeled, chunked

3 large carrots, peeled, cut in 1-1/2 inch pieces, steamed

1 turnip, peeled, cut in eighths, steamed

1 rutabaga, peeled, cut in eighths, steamed

1/2 pound brussels sprouts, steamed and halved, optional

4 tablespoons olive or vegetable oil, butter, or a combination

1 tablespoon prepared horseradish, or to taste

2 tablespoons cider vinegar

1 teaspoon dill, or to taste

Salt and pepper, to taste

1. Put cooked vegetables in a large bowl.

2. Heat remaining ingredients and toss with vegetables. Adjust seasoning. Serve warm, room temperature or cold.

NOTE: Vegetables should be just soft, not overcooked.

ZUCCHINI, TOMATOES AND EGGPLANT

Serves 6

◆ Summer is the perfect time for this casserole of fresh vegetables. Make the dish ahead and serve it warm or cold with grilled meats or eggs. Vary the proportions according to taste.

1 pound zucchini, cut in

1/2-inch slices

2 onions, thinly sliced

1 medium eggplant, cubed

1 green pepper, thinly sliced

1 pound fresh tomatoes, peeled,

seeded, chopped

2 to 3 cloves garlic, pressed

1 heaping teaspoon dried thyme,

oregano, basil or a blend, or use

fresh herbs, to taste

4 tablespoons olive oil

Salt and pepper, to taste

2 tablespoons fresh parsley,

chopped

1/4 cup black olives, chopped,

optional

1. Put all ingredients, except parsley and olives, into a large casserole.

2. Cover and cook in a preheated 325 degree oven for about 1 hour, stirring occasionally. Vegetables should be soft. Taste and correct seasoning.

3. Or, cook it on the stove in a large pot about 45 minutes to 1 hour on medium low heat, stirring occasionally. Taste and correct seasoning.

4. Dish also can be cooked in the microwave oven according to manufacturer's instructions.

5. Serve warm with a sprinkling of Parmesan cheese, chopped parsley or olives. Or serve cold without cheese.

GLOSSARY OF TERMS AND TECHNIQUES

ADJUST SEASONING: Same as correct seasoning.

BAKE: Cook covered or uncovered in dry heat, usually an oven.

BASTE: Spoon or brush fat or liquid over cooking food to moisten and flavor.

BEAT: Mix rapidly to include air and make smooth with a spoon, fork, electric beater or wire whisk.

BLANCH: Precook an ingredient (usually a vegetable or meat) in a pot of boiling water for a minute, more or less, depending upon the size of the ingredient. Immediately drain and rinse under cold water to stop the cooking. Blanching or parboiling mean the same. Use to loosen skins of fruits and vegetables, leach salt and fat from meat, or precook vegetables ahead of time.

BLEND: Combine well two or more ingredients.

BOIL: Liquid heated to make big rolling bubbles.

CORRECT SEASONING: Taste food as it cooks and before it's served. Add a dash of whatever seasoning needed to make the dish taste right to you. Also referred to as **ADJUST SEASONING**.

BRAISE: Brown ingredient with a little liquid, cover and slowly cook.

BROIL: Cook with direct heat, usually in oven.

CHOP: Cut in small pieces.

DASH: Small amount, few drops.

DONE: When food can be removed from cooking heat. For meats and poultry, usually when pinkness disappears; for fish, when it barely flakes. Use your finger to press meat: it's rare if the meat is soft, and well done if it's hard to the touch.

FOLD: Gently combine a light ingredient with a heavier one, with up-and-down strokes, by hand rather than with a mixer.

GREASE AND FLOUR: Prepare baking pan by lightly rubbing with butter or oil, then sprinkling with flour and shaking pan so flour clings.

GRILL: Cook over direct heat, as on a barbecue.

MINCE: Chop very fine.

POACH: Gently cook in simmering liquid.

PRESS: A clove of garlic squeezed in a small gadget (a garlic press) that squashes it to pulp.

PUREE: Mash until smooth.

SIMMER: Heat liquid so it makes few, if any, bubbles for gentle or long cooking.

SKIM: Remove fat with a spoon.

STEAM: Cook in a basket or on a rack suspended above boiling water or liquid.

STIR-FRY: Cook bite-size pieces of food in a skillet or wok on a high heat. Food is constantly tossed so it cooks quickly and evenly.

TASTE: Try food as it cooks so seasoning can be adjusted to preference.

ZEST: Thin outer peel of citrus fruit, not including white inner layer. Use a fine grater, a gadget called a zester or vegetable peeler to shear the outer layer, then finely mince.

BASIC SUBSTITUTIONS AND EQUIVALENTS

GINGER, 1/2 teaspoon grated fresh = 1/4 teaspoon ground ginger

GARLIC, 1 clove = 1/8 teaspoon garlic powder

ONION, 1 medium = 2 teaspoons onion powder

ONION, 1/4 cup diced = 1 tablespoon instant minced onion

PARSLEY, 2 tablespoons minced fresh = 1 tablespoon parsley flakes

LEMON, 1 fresh = 2 to 3 tablespoons juice, 2 teaspoons zest or grated peel

LEMON, zest of 1 fresh or 1 teaspoon grated fresh peel = 1 teaspoon grated dry peel

ORANGE, 1 fresh = 6 to 8 tablespoons juice, or 4 to 5 tablespoons reconstituted frozen juice

ORANGE, zest of 1 fresh or 1 teaspoon grated fresh peel = 1 teaspoon grated dry peel

LEMON JUICE, 1 teaspoon = 1/2 teaspoon vinegar

MILK, 1 cup = 1/2 cup evaporated plus 1/2 cup water

MILK, 1 cup = 1/3 cup nonfat dry plus 1 cup water

MILK, 1 cup = 1 cup fruit juice

MILK, 1 cup = 1 cup water plus 2 teaspoons butter

BUTTERMILK OR SOUR MILK, 1 cup = 1 cup milk plus 1 tablespoon white vinegar (or lemon juice) left to sit for 5 minutes

FLOUR, 2 tablespoons (for thickening) = 1 tablespoon cornstarch, rice or potato starch, or arrowroot

---

FLOUR, 7/8 cup all-purpose = 1 cup cake flour

BAKING POWDER, 1 teaspoon = 1/4 teaspoon baking soda plus 1/2 cup yogurt or buttermilk

---

BAKING POWDER, 1 teaspoon = Scant 1/2 teaspoon baking soda plus 1/2 teaspoon cream of tartar

---

CHOCOLATE, 1 square, unsweetened = 3 tablespoons unsweetened cocoa plus 1 tablespoon butter or oil

---

HONEY, 1 cup = 1-1/4 cups sugar plus 1/4 cup liquid

EGGS, 1 whole = 2 yolks for thickening

BUTTER, 1 stick, 1/4 pound = 1/2 cup or 8 tablespoons

WHIPPING CREAM, 1/2 pint, 1 cup = 2 cups whipped

CHEESE (cheddar, jack, Swiss), 4 ounces = 1 cup shredded

MEASUREMENTS

3 teaspoons = 1 tablespoon
4 tablespoons = 1/4 cup
16 tablespoons = 1 cup or 8 fluid ounces
2 cups = 16 fluid ounces or 1 pint
4 cups = 2 pints or 1 quart
1 liter = 1.06 quarts
4 quarts = 1 gallon

SAMPLE SHOPPING LIST FOR FOUR—ONE WEEK

◆ This sample shopping list assumes condiments, herbs, spices, and oils are on hand. Use the list as a guide. Substitute foods according to individual budget and dietary needs. To shop for one or two, cut the proportions in half. Prices will vary depending on season, availability, and weekly store specials. (Those below reflect 1991 average spring prices in California supermarkets.)

PRODUCE

Bananas, 3 pounds: $1
Tomatoes, 2 pounds: $.80
Apples, 3 pounds: $1.50
Broccoli, 1 pound: $.69
Cabbage, 3 pounds: $1
Lettuce, 3 heads: $1
Spinach, 3 bunches: $1
Radishes, 3 bunches: $1
Green Onion, 3 bunches: $1
Carrots, 4 pounds: $1
Cucumber, 1: $.49
Celery, 1 bunch: $.69
Zucchini, 2 pounds: $1
Ginger, 1/8 pound: $.40

Bean sprouts, 1/2 pound: $.30
Grapefruit, 5 pounds: $1.49
Garlic, 1/8 pound: $.40
Potatoes, 10 pounds: $1.69
Onions, 3 pounds: $1
Lemons, 4: $1
Corn, 5 ears: $1
Mushrooms, 1/4 pound: $.50
TOTAL: $19.95

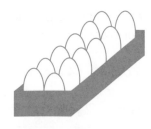

DAIRY

Jack cheese, 2 pounds: $3.99
Longhorn, 1 pound: $2.50
Cream cheese, 1/2 pound: $.95
Margarine, 1 pound: $.79
Nonfat milk, 2 gallons: $4
Plain yogurt, 2 pounds: $1.45
Eggs, 2-1/2 dozen: $2.80
Butter, 1 pound: $1.69
TOTAL: $18.17

MEAT

Whole fryers, 2 ($.69/pound): $4.25
Package, 7 legs and thighs
($.89/pound): $3.50
Leg of lamb ($2.69/pound): $8.00
Fresh snapper, 1 pound: $3.29
Frozen whole turkey
($.79/pound): $11.17
Bacon, low sodium, 1 pound: $1.99
Ground beef, 1-1/2 pounds: $2.25
TOTAL: $34.45

BREADS, GRAINS

Look for many of these items in
bulk foods sections.

Quaker Oats, 2-1/2 pounds: $3.29
Corn Flakes, 18 ounces: $2.09
Popcorn, 2 pounds: $1.09
Flour, 5 pounds: $1.19
Sugar, 5 pounds: $1.99
Graham Crackers: $2.59
Ritz Crackers, 1 pound: $2.09
Bread, 3 pounds: $2.50
Pita bread, 1 package: $1.69
Rice cakes, 2 packages: $1.98
Tortillas, 3 dozen: $.99
Dried white beans, 1 pound: $.67

Fettucini, 1 pound: $1.09
Egg noodles, 1 pound: $1.07
Rice, 5 pounds: $2.17
Crackers, 1 package: $1.49
TOTAL: $27.98

FROZEN

Apple juice, 12-ounce can: $1.15
Orange juice, 16-ounce can: $2.15
Peas, 2 pounds: $1.89
Corn, 2 pounds: $1.85
TOTAL: $7.04

STAPLES

Peanut butter, 36 ounces: $5.29
Raisins, 1 pound: $1.49
Tomato sauce, 3 8-ounce cans: $.89
Applesauce, 32 ounces: $1.59
TOTAL: $9.26

**GRAND TOTAL:
$116.85**

INDEX